Math Problem Solving in Action

In this new book from popular math consultant and bestselling author Dr. Nicki Newton, you'll learn how to help students in grades K–2 become more effective and confident problem solvers. Problem solving is a necessary skill for the 21st century but can be overwhelming for both teachers and students alike. Dr. Nicki shows how to make word problems more engaging and fun, starting in the early elementary grades so that students have a strong foundation to build upon.

Topics include:

- Using games, songs, and poems to make complex mathematical concepts more accessible;
- Showing students how to reason about, model, and discuss word problems;
- Implementing problem-solving workshops and workstations to maximize practice time and encourage collaboration;
- Teaching students to recognize and apply elementary mathematical concepts—including addition, subtraction, part-whole relationships, etc.—in real-life situations;
- Incorporating different types of assessment to measure student progress and help them get to the next level.

Each chapter offers examples, charts, and tools that you can use immediately. The book also features a set of action plans so you can move forward with confidence and implement the book's ideas in your own classroom.

Dr. Nicki Newton has been an educator for 28 years, working both nationally and internationally, with students of all ages. She has worked on developing Math Workshop and Guided Math Institutes around the country; visit her website at www.drnickinewton.com. She is also an avid blogger (www.guidedmath.wordpress.com), tweeter (@drnickimath) and Pinterest pinner (www.pinterest.com/drnicki7).

Math Problem Solving in Action

Getting Students to Love Word Problems, Grades K–2

Dr. Nicki Newton

Routledge
Taylor & Francis Group

NEW YORK AND LONDON

First published 2018
by Routledge
711 Third Avenue, New York, NY 10017

and by Routledge
2 Park Square, Milton Park, Abingdon, Oxon, OX14 4RN

Routledge is an imprint of the Taylor & Francis Group, an informa business

© 2018 Taylor & Francis

Library of Congress Cataloging-in-Publication Data
A catalog record for this book has been requested

ISBN: 978-1-138-05646-6 (hbk)
ISBN: 978-1-138-05453-0 (pbk)
ISBN: 978-1-315-16533-2 (ebk)

Typeset in Palatino
by Apex CoVantage, LLC

Dedication

I dedicate this book to Gregory County (beloved uncle).

Contents

Foreword

Over the course of my 13 years as a grade 5 teacher and now in my third year as a Math Coach, I have witnessed the same situation over and over—a student diligently works on an assignment practicing a skill she has been taught and then she gets to about the 10th question and her brain freezes. Her brow furrows as she attempts to make sense of what she is seeing. She has no idea what to do. She is so confused, she finally gets out of her seat and approaches her teacher for help saying, "I don't get it." I can predict which kind of question it is: the first word problem that appears on the assignment. In conversation after conversation with parents, teachers, and my pre-service teacher students, people relate to me their horror stories of their childhood math education and their feelings of being inept as they tried to solve word problems. They hated them and, in many cases, developed anxiety and even phobias surrounding math.

Traditionally, word problems have provided a challenge for students. In our efforts to help students be successful, we have tried to develop methods to make the process easier for them. I can vividly remember my years as a classroom teacher and how I would administer my unit tests. There was a colorful poster on the wall with each operation in bold letters. Beneath each operation, there were all the keywords students should look for to know which operation they would need to do in order to solve the problem. As I read the test out loud to the students (so I could be sure I was assessing their math ability and not their reading ability), I would pause every few sentences and have them highlight all the numbers and any of the keywords they could see so that when they were working independently they could focus in on those items. I know. I'm cringing, too, as I type this. This is just so far away from what I now understand is the best way to teach students to solve word problems.

Even though my methods those days did nothing to help my students' conceptual understanding, reasoning, or problem-solving ability, my students were generally successful in solving the word problems they were presented with because typically the problem types given to them all had the results unknown. So, finding the key word of "altogether" meant that they should add the numbers in the problem together. Students computed the answer, I put a big "C" on their correct answers and we all moved forward thinking they had successfully moved forward on their math journey. The problem is, they only learned to be, as Graham Fletcher said in a webinar I experienced recently, "pluckers." I had trained them to pluck the numbers out of the word problem, find a keyword to determine an operation and then compute the answer.

Consider this word problem:

> There were 6 birds in a tree. Some more flew in. Now there are 9 birds in the tree altogether. How many birds flew in?

I would be willing to bet that in my classroom years ago, more students than I would have imagined would have seen the numbers 6 and 9 and the word "altogether" and thought they needed to add them together. They would have given the answer of 15 and not looked back. In my attempt to make students successful in math, I did nothing to help them understand the situation in the word problem. So while my methods got them through that test and math topic, I was not preparing them for the future.

My first exposure to the existence of different problem types was several years ago when I attended a two-day conference focusing on what was, at the time, the "new Common Core standards" in Math and English Language Arts. One of the first sessions I chose to attend was a math session led by Dr. Nicki Newton. I vividly remember learning from her about open and double number lines, strategies to solve computation problems in ways other than the traditional algorithms, and the idea that there were several problem types for various operations in which various parts of the situation could be unknown and not just the result. My mind was blown. Those ideas had never appeared in any books I read in my teacher preparatory classes or the textbook I had been using to teach my students. Dr. Nicki opened my mind to a whole new way of understanding mathematics. I changed my session choices for the rest of the conference and stayed with her in all her sessions.

The word problem types in the Common Core State Standards are based on the revolutionary work by Thomas P. Carpenter, Elizabeth Fennema, Megan Loef Franke, Susan Empson, and Linda Levi in their book *Cognitively Guided Instruction*. They share that research has shown that students are much more successful in math when they understand the underlying structure of word problems. No longer should we think of word problems as being defined by one operation such as an "addition" or "subtraction" word problem. Instead, the authors demonstrate the need for us to help our students understand the basic structure of the word problems. The benefit of this is that these structures will remain the same during many years of their math journeys with the only difference being the numbers they are asked to use to compute numerical answers. In kindergarten they begin with numbers within 10, but by grade 5 they are asked to use multi-digit numbers, fractions, and decimals. Yet, the problem types remain the same.

There are three other benefits of our work on understanding the problem types and additionally having students model the situations. First, once students have created a model for the situation, they aren't limited to one operation to solve the problem. In the above example with 6 birds in a tree, some more flying in, and there being 9 birds in the tree, one student might decide to subtract 6 from 9 to get 3, but another student might start at 6 and think about what they can add to it to arrive at 9. This flexibility of thought is exactly the goal embedded in our philosophies of teaching early numeracy concepts to our students. Not only will students develop the ability to think critically about the word problem situations, but their models will enable them to the second benefit: being able to visualize the inverse relationship between addition and subtraction. Finally, by using a question mark for the unknown in the models of the word problem, we are setting the foundation for algebraic thinking since further on their math journey the "?" will be replaced with a variable.

This can certainly seem like an overwhelming undertaking, but thankfully Dr. Nicki has created this comprehensive resource that provides all that you need to embark on this critical journey. This book is an invaluable resource that you will want to keep close at hand. She is with you every step of the way as she provides explanations of the problem types, strategies, and models that can be used to teach our young students these various problem types. With Dr. Nicki's guidance, you will be creating classrooms of students who will feel confident when they see word problems and, with a smile on their faces, will get out of their seats to confidently share their work. You will be providing them with the foundation of mathematical understanding that will not only help them through the content in their current grade level, but for future grade levels as well. We owe it to our students to teach these word problem types and, in the process, create a generation of lifelong mathematicians!

Ann Elise Record

Reference

Carpenter, T. P., Fennema, E., Franke, M. L., Levi, L., and Empson, S. B. (2014). *Children's mathematics: Cognitively guided instruction* (2nd ed.). Portsmouth, NH: Heinemann.

Meet the Author

Dr. Nicki Newton has been an educator for 28 years, working both nationally and internationally, with students of all ages. Having spent the first part of her career as a literacy and social studies specialist, she built on those frameworks to inform her math work. She believes that math is intricately intertwined with reading, writing, listening, and speaking. She has worked on developing math workshop and guided math institutes around the country. Most recently, she has been helping districts and schools nationwide to integrate their State Standards for Mathematics and think deeply about how to teach these within a Math Workshop Model.

Dr. Nicki works with teachers, coaches, and administrators to make math come alive by considering the powerful impact of building a community of mathematicians that make meaning of real math together. When students do real math, they learn it, they own it, they understand it, and they can do it. Every one of them.

Dr. Nicki's website is www.drnickinewton.com. She is also an avid blogger (www.guidedmath.wordpress.com), tweeter (@drnickimath), and Pinterest pinner (www.pinterest.com/drnicki7).

Acknowledgments

I am so excited and honored to be writing this book. I love word problems, and I want all students to love them too. I could not have done this book without the help of others. So many people have helped me to write this book. My family is always there, encouraging me along the way—Marvin, Sharon, Tia, Uncle Bill, Clinese, all my nieces, nephews and great nieces and nephews and cousins. My friends always support my efforts (Kimberly, Tracie, Tammy, Demorris, Terri and Scott, Alison and Ann). My best assistant ever—Brittany! We have several people who help us as well, including Anna, Nancy, Gabby and Debbie. I am very grateful to Ann Elise who wrote the foreword for the book. My editor Lauren is fantastic, patient, and only the best editor ever! I am forever thankful and grateful to all the teachers and students that I work with throughout the journey. You all make it possible. I sincerely thank everyone named and unnamed who has helped in the process.

Introduction

Problem Solving Should Prepare Students for the Future

Getting little kids to solve big word problems is a huge undertaking. It should be educational, engaging and downright fun! There are so many possibilities. It gives us a reason to bring back Play-Doh, puppets and felt figures. See, problem solving must be accessible to students so they get it! Oh, and they can definitely get it if you tell stories that pertain to their lives. In the primary grades, we have a great opportunity because the students haven't learned to hate word problems yet! With a firm foundation, they can actually learn to look forward to doing them and, I dare say, learn to LOVE them!

Problem solving is about thinking, reasoning, exploring, hypothesizing and wondering. It takes dedication and perseverance. It takes "being up for the challenge." It's delicate. There are many aspects. One aspect is word problems. I am writing this book about *how to get all kids **to love** word problems* because I truly believe it is possible. But I don't think we will ever achieve it if we keep doing what we've been doing.

We are working with students from 2 different generations in the primary grades. The first group is Generation Z and Alpha Gen. "Generation Z (also known as Post-Millennials, the iGeneration, Plurals or the Homeland Generation)" (Wikipedia, 2017) is the first generation to be born into a world where the internet has always existed.

> They are the first truly mobile-first generation, so they place a big emphasis on **personalization and relevance** . . . Whereas Millennials use three screens on average, Gen Zers **use five:** a smartphone, TV, laptop, desktop and iPod/iPad. . . . The average Gen Zer has the **attention span of about 8 seconds** . . .
> www.cmo.com/articles/2015/6/11/15-mind-blowing-stats-about-generation-z.html

Furthermore GenZers are "extremely social and group oriented . . . prefer game-like learning situations . . . they place a value on the speed of their work, not accuracy" (Phillip, 2015).

They will work with people from around the world from the chairs in their home. They will need to solve problems daily. Most of what they will do, we have yet to imagine. But what we know for sure is that they will need to know how to think out loud, explain and justify their reasoning to others and represent their thinking. So, we have to take problem solving seriously and do it often. Thomas Frey, one of the top futurist researchers in the world notes that "the top three skills needed for the future [are] adaptability, flexibility and resourcefulness" (Frey, 2014).

Given what we know, what are we doing in schools? Why do we teach students word problems? What are we trying to accomplish? Do we want students to actually learn something or are we engaging in raging acts of futility? We should be considering our students within their lived realities and teaching them to thrive in a future we can't name. Do we tap into the need for personalization and relevance? How often do we integrate technology into the teaching of problem solving? Do we allow them many opportunities to work in groups and play games around problem solving? Do we set up learning opportunities that require them to be adaptable, flexible and resourceful?

So, I have written this book to talk about ways to think about teaching word problems. There are 12 Chapters.

Part I: Introduction to Word Problems

Chapter 1: Play-Doh®, Puppets and Other Real Stuff Make Problems Make Sense

Chapter 2: Problem Solving in Math Workshop

Chapter 3: The Basic Framework

Part II: A Deeper Dive

Chapter 4: Add To Problems
    A. Problem type
    B. Models
    C. Assessment

Chapter 5: Take From Problems
    A. Problem type
    B. Models
    C. Assessment

Chapter 6: Part-Part-Whole Problems
    A. Problem type
    B. Models
    C. Assessment

Chapter 7: Compare Problems
    A. Problem type
    B. Models
    C. Assessment

Chapter 8: Two-Step Problems and More
  A. Problem type
  B. Models
  C. Assessment

Chapter 9: Problem Solving Across Math Topics

Part III: Other Word Problems

Chapter 10: Reasoning about Problems

Chapter 11: Springboards into Great Word Problem Premises: *Math Mentor Texts, Poems, Songs, Shared Experiences and Games*

> This chapter is about teaching in ways that students love. This chapter is about doing some fun stuff. This chapter is about remembering that we teach children who love animals, songs, books and stories.

Chapter 12: Action Plan

> In this chapter we focus on the next steps. It's important to write an action plan. It's important to outline tasks and set dates to move the work forward. Change requires action.

Word problems can be great! Word problems are the stuff life is made of. If we can make connections for children between their daily lives and the problems we pose and solve in school, we will have much more success. This book is about giving students a repertoire of tools, models and strategies to help them think about, understand and solve word problems. We want to scaffold reasoning opportunities from the concrete (using objects) to the pictorial (pictures and drawings) and, finally, to the abstract (writing equations).

Dr. Nicki Newton

References

Frey, T. (2014). "101 Endangered Jobs by 2030." FuturistSpeaker.com. Retrieved from http://www.futuristspeaker. com/2014/11/101-endangered-jobs-by-2030/

"Generation Z." (2017). Wikipedia. Retrieved from https://en.wikipedia. org/wiki/Generation_Z

Phillip, M. (2015). "21 Facts About Generation Z That You Need to Know." Thrivist.com. Retrieved from http://thrivist. com/21-facts-about-generation-z-that-you-need-to-know/

Part I

Introduction to Word Problems

1

Play-Doh®, Puppets and Other Real Stuff Make Problems Make Sense

Play-Doh Matters

Start with Play-Doh! I guarantee that you will immediately have your students' attention. Next add puppets. You'll have them at *Go!* Continue with other real stuff (like stickers, toy cars and marbles) and students will start to *love* word problems. They will associate them with doing fun stuff. Fun is always a great hook! Although researchers have found that story problems "are notoriously difficult to solve" (Cummins, Kintsh, Reusser and Weimer, 1988), I argue they don't have to be. The way that we currently teach them is often off-putting to students. We have to shift how we are doing things. Really, more than shift, we need to go back to what we used to do (over 30 years ago).

Students grow to hate problem solving by 3rd grade. But it should be presented as a challenge. Students should look forward to working with word problems because it's the stuff they do every day. We simply have to *mathematize* the stuff they do every day. Students should own the problems they solve and pose. They should solve problems about their families, their friends, their daily activities, their school and their lives. If the problems made sense to the students, then students could make sense of the problems.

Wording Matters

Wording matters. There is a famous example of how students understand the meaning of problems but how sometimes the language gets in the way. Hudson (1983) posed this problem to some children: "There are 5 birds and 3 worms. How many more birds are there than worms?" Many of the children could not solve the problem. However, when the problem was reworded, "How many birds won't get a worm?" many of the students could solve the problem. Riley, Greeno and Heller (1983) said that rewording helps students to understand the problem, and when students understand the problem, they can solve it. Cummins (1991) pointed out that "the data seem to indicate that the knowledge [to solve problems] is there, but is simply is not accessed when problems are worded in certain ways" (p. 267). She argues that students fail to do so because they are missing or "have inadequate mappings of verbal expressions to part-whole structures". She maintains that "rewording enhances performance."

So for example, if we say, "There are 8 kids and 5 cupcakes. How many more kids are there than cupcakes?", students are puzzled. But, if you say, "There are 8 kids and 5 cupcakes. How many kids don't get a cupcake?", the students will say 3. If you say, "How many more cupcakes do we need so that everybody gets one?", the students know the answer. See, this pertains to their everyday lives. They fully understand this scenario and have no trouble reasoning about it. After the understanding is there, the teacher can scaffold the problem with the academic language. There are more kids than cupcakes. There are fewer cupcakes than kids.

Scaffolding Matters

Templates scaffold the process. Pólya (1957) first laid out the process for us with his problem-solving questions with his 4 phases (see Figure 1.1). Templates build on Pólya's original phases (see Figure 1.2). They help to scaffold the thinking and, with use over time, the students begin to internalize the process. Eventually, the templates are phased out. Have anchor charts up that talk about the process of problem solving. Also, have the students make their own mini anchor charts. Once the template use is phased out, still have the students sketch out the template into their problem-solving notebooks. When students are organized they are much more likely to succeed.

Three Types of Templates

Templates should be used in a gradual release cycle. I do, we do, you do. See Figures 1.2, 1.3 and 1.4 for examples.

Figure 1.1

Understand the Problem
Discuss the problem.
State what is known.
State what you are looking for.
Comprehend what is happening in it.
Visualize the problem
(make a picture in your head).
Retell the story.
Sketch it out (quick draw for 30 seconds).
Translate it in your own words.
What's important?
What people, places and things stand out?
What numbers are given?

Devise a Plan
Which way will you solve it?

Carry Out a Plan
Do the math.
Check the work.

Looking Back
Think about your answer.
Does it make sense?

Source: Pólya (1957)

Figure 1.2 is a fully scaffolded template.

Figure 1.2

Tom had 5 marbles. He gave 2 of them to his brother. How many marbles does he have left?

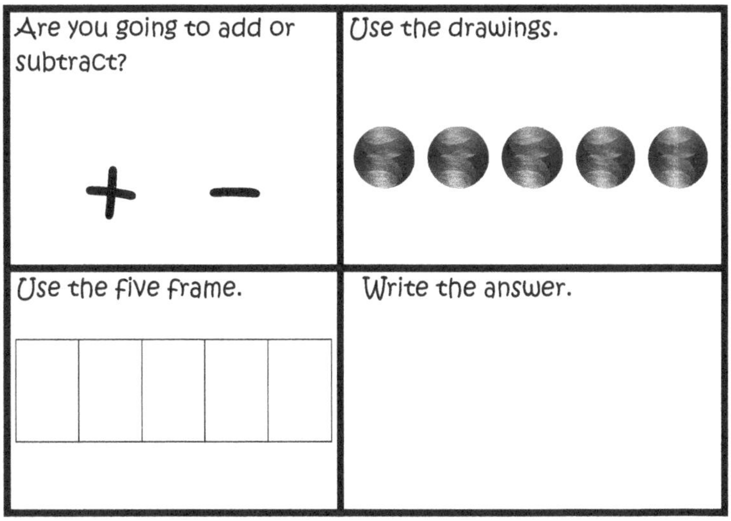

Are you going to add or subtract?	Use the drawings.
$+$ $-$	
Use the five frame.	Write the answer.

Figure 1.3 is a partially scaffolded template. The students get to choose.

Figure 1.3

The bakery made 5 cupcakes. Then they made 5 more. How many did they make altogether? Choose 2 ways to solve the problem from the idea mat.

Are you going to add or subtract? **+** —	Draw a picture.
Use the 10 frame. 	Use counters.

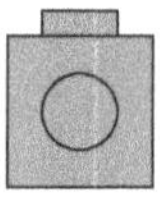

Use a number line:

1 2 3 4 5 6 7 8 9 10

Fill in the number sentence

_____ + _____ = _____

Answer: _____ cupcakes

Figure 1.4 is an unscaffolded template. This template is more of an idea bank with strategies and models that students can choose from.

Figure 1.4

Model your thinking (open number line, table, diagram, picture).	Write the number sentence that shows what we are looking for. Solve it. Show answer with units.
Explain your thinking. Talk about your strategies.	Solve the problem another way.

Models Matter

Students need to be able to explain and discuss how they are representing the problem. What models are they using specifically? I define a model as how students are showing their thinking about the problem. This is different than a strategy, which is what they are doing with the numbers. Oftentimes, these words get used interchangeably, but I think it is important to have students explain both what their model is and what their strategy is. Therefore, in the examples in the word problem type chapters, I have shown various models and discussed various strategies.

In terms of models, there are 3 categories: concrete, pictorial and abstract. Concrete models can be cubes, tiles, bears, or any type of real object (marbles, dolls, toy cars, etc.). Pictorial models are drawings or sketches. Students are encouraged to use sketches because these are quick and to the point, whereas drawings can take quite some time (like 10 minutes to draw a marble). So teach the children to do sketches so they can get on with the business of problem solving. The sketch is just a tool to use for thinking. Abstract models include number grids, number lines and tape diagrams.

There are so many types of models, but most state standards name the ones that students must absolutely know at particular grade levels. Most state standards are now putting a heavy emphasis on tape diagrams and number lines (both marked and open). It is important for students to have toolkits with both concrete tools, sketch paper and templates. Templates are also a tool for thinking (number frames, number bonds, part-part whole mats, cube pictures, etc.).

Strategies Matter

Students need to be able to explain how they are thinking about the numbers. Are they counting on, counting up or using known facts? What exactly are they doing with the numbers and can they explain it? Does it make sense? Are they using the facts that they are learning? Because what good does it do for students to learn their doubles facts and then never use them when solving problems? So it is important for teachers and students to talk about the strategies they are using and how we use different strategies for different problems so that we can be efficient problem solvers.

Perseverance Matters

One of the most important things that students need to know about problem solving is that they have to *persevere* with the problems. They need to get the idea that they have to stick with it and can't give up. There should be mini-lessons around perseverance. There are so many ways to teach and talk about this now. There are videos, picture books, songs and posters (see www.pinterest.com/drnicki7/growth-mindsetperseverance/). There are several great videos. *Sesame Street* has done some great videos for the primary grades, including *Don't Give Up* featuring Bruno Mars and the Muppets, as well as *The Power of Yet* featuring Janelle Monáe and the Muppets.

Questioning Matters

Good questions are the building blocks of good problem solving. We shouldn't ever give answers. We should only scaffold thinking with good questions (see Figure 1.5). When a child says they don't know, always

Figure 1.5

Problem-Solving Questions	
Visualize	If this were a commercial, what would you see?
Summarize	What is this problem about? Do you understand the problem?
Write the Set-Up Equation	What are we looking for? What is missing? How will you write that equation?
Make a Plan	What type of problem is this? How many steps is it going to take to solve this problem? What is your plan?
Solve One Way	How are you going to solve this problem? What models will you use? What strategies will you use?
Check Another	How are you going to check this problem? Did you use numbers, drawings, diagrams, tables or acting out to solve this problem?
Double-Double Check	Did you check the math and the answer? Does the answer make sense?
Explain Your Thinking	Did you write down what you did?
Think About the Thinking Of Others	Who did it the way John did? Who did it a different way? Who agrees with John? Does anybody disagree with John?
Scaffolding Questions	What tool could you use to solve this problem? What template could you use to help solve this problem? What model could you use to solve this problem? What strategy could you use to solve this problem?

ask them to look in their toolkit (an actual one with tools appropriate to the grade) or use a template (an actual one that is part of their toolkits). Never ask someone else to help because the minute you do this, you just taught the child who had the question that they don't have to persevere. You have in essence said, "Don't stick with it. I'll send someone in to save you." You didn't intentionally say it, but that is the message received. This is how students learn helplessness. Instead, when a child says they are stuck, say, "What could you use to help?" If you need to, suggest a starting point. But never overscaffold. Sometimes teachers will say, "Take out the 10 frames. Now put 4 on the top and 3 on the bottom. Now how many do you have altogether?" Okay—if you do that you are *guilty of overscaffolding*. Don't overscaffold. Let your students think. Let them wrestle with the problem. Let them figure out that they can figure it out!

Key Points

- Play-Doh Matters
- Wording Matters
- Scaffolding Matters
- Perseverance Matters
- Questioning Matters

Summary

Problem solving is about helping students to see how math is part of our everyday lives. The goal is to foster flexibility, competence and confidence. Since the process is involved, problems should relate to everyday life so that they make sense to the students. Teachers need to word problems in ways that build conceptual understanding. Templates help to scaffold access to all the moving parts of the problem from the beginning to the end. Perseverance should be explicitly taught so that students learn to stick with it when they get stuck. Good questions are powerful tools to scaffold student work around problem solving.

Reflection Questions

1. Do you use real-life stuff when you teach problem solving?
2. Do you carefully choose the wording so that students understand the problem?
3. Do you use templates to scaffold the process?
4. Do you teach perseverance explicitly?
5. What is your big takeaway from this chapter? What one thing in your teaching will you start or expand?

References

Cummins, D. (1991). Children's interpretations of arithmetic word problems. *Cognition and Instruction, 8*(3), 261–289.

Cummins, D. D., Kintsh, W., Reusser, K., and Weimer, R. (1988). The role of understanding in solving word problems. *Cognitive Psychology, 20*(4), 405–438.

Hudson, T. (1983). Correspondences and numerical differences between disjoint sets. *Child Development, 54*(1), 84–90.

Pólya, G. (1957). *How to solve it: A new aspect of mathematical method.* Garden City, NY: Doubleday.

Riley, M. S., Greeno, J. G., and Heller, J. I. (1983). Development of children's problem-solving ability in arithmetic. In H. P. Ginsberg (Ed.), *The development of mathematical thinking* (pp. 153–196). Orlando, FL: Academic.

2

Problem Solving in Math Workshop

Problem solving should be done every day as a whole class routine (see Figure 2.1). It should also be done in small guided math groups and math workstations. When done in whole groups, the emphasis is on developing the habits of mind and ways of doing that good problem solvers need. The focus here is not on quickly solving a problem but on going through the process of problem solving. It is a practice that is developed over time. Great problem solving is interwoven throughout the math block (see Figure 2.1).

Figure 2.1

Element	When	How? What does it look like?
Problem of the Day (word problems)	Every day some work on the problem (this is longer, around 10 minutes)	Every day students take out their math problem-solving notebooks and work on their problems.
Energizers and Routines	Every day (these are short)	Reasoning activities What doesn't belong? True or false?
Guided Math Groups	A few times a week	Differentiated based on student needs
Math Workstations	Daily (students should go to the problem-solving station every day or almost every day)	Differentiated based on student needs Activities vary—solving problems, writing problems, sorting problems, matching problems and equations
Homework	A weekly problem-solving packet	2–3 rich tasks around the current unit of study with maybe one review problem
Source: Adapted from Gojak (2011, p. 29)		

Problem Solving in Whole Groups: Rethinking Problem of the Day

Scenario: The students come to the rug and sit criss-cross applesauce waiting for Mrs. Chi to pull up the word problem on the interactive board. The problem says:

There were 5 students upstairs and 5 students downstairs. How many students were there altogether?

Mrs. Chi asks the students to make a picture in their head of this problem. She then says "Who wants to tell us what you saw." Brandon explains that he saw the school. There were 5 kids upstairs and 5 downstairs. Mrs. Chi asks if someone can come up and write the set-up equation. Lisa volunteers. Mrs. Chi then asks who has a plan of how we might model this problem. Marta says we need to use the Rekenrek. So, Mrs. Chi pulls up the virtual Rekenrek on the interactive board and calls up Timmy to model the problem. Everyone agrees with Timmy's model, and they agree that the answer is 10. (The class ends problem solving for the day but agrees to continue with this problem tomorrow). The next day Mrs. Chi asks the students to solve the problem another way just to be double sure. What could they use? Jamal says they could draw it. He then models on his white board a picture of a 2 story house with 5 kids upstairs and 5 kids downstairs. He got 10 and everyone agrees with him. Mrs. Chi says that we need to check the math and then check that we answered the question. When all of that is done, the children move on to the mini-lesson for the day.

The Problem of the Day is often an exercise in answer-getting. Students are given a problem, a bit of time to work through it and then the answer is discussed. I propose we do something radically different. That we don't rush to the answer. That we do what Phil Daro says: "Delay answer-getting" (2016). Sometimes, even give the students the answer so that part is done. Then, focus on the process of problem solving. Rather than a *problem of the day*, consider it more of like a *problem of the week*.

Students get the problem the first day, they read it, visualize it and discuss it with partners, in small groups and together with the whole class. The initial emphasis is to get everyone to understand the problem. In order to do this, they need to *visualize and summarize* the problem. That means that they need to make a picture of the problem in their head and then talk about what that picture looks like. As part of the whole-class routine, students should share out their thinking and then discuss that thinking to see if everyone agrees on what the problem is about. That might be all they do on day one.

The next thing the students should decide is what type of problem it is and what they are looking for. Students should write a set-up equation with a question mark or letter for the unknown part. It is important that students can identify exactly what they are looking for and that they write a set-up equation. Students should just use the letters of the things that they are working with. For example, if the problem is about marbles, then the students use an M to designate the unknown.

The next thing students should do is make a written plan rather than simply picking some numbers and jumping into the problem to find an answer. The practice of thinking about the problem and really deciding what it is about is powerful. Students should write what they are going to do and then do that. After they have solved one way, they should always be encouraged to check by another. This might take two or three days.

It is important for students to be able to make connections between different representations of the problem, such as equations, verbal descriptions, tables, graphs, sketches and diagrams (NCTM, 2000; NGA Center, 2010). They should always read the work of others to see if it makes sense, and if it doesn't, they should have the language to challenge each other or ask for clarification.

The next thing students should do is double-double-check their work. I have found that when teachers tell students to check their work, they tend to check the math. The math could be correct and the answer wrong. For example, 3 plus 3 is 6, but it might have been a subtraction problem. So, ask students to check the math and check to see if the answer makes sense. In order to do all of this and to do it well, students should use the templates that were discussed in chapter 1 (see more with Figures 1.3, 1.4 and 1.5).

Problem Solving in Guided Math Groups

*Scenario: The children rush to the guided math table giggling because they see Play-Doh. They sit down very excitedly and very wiggly. I tell them that our agenda for the day is to work on subtraction word problems. I tell them that the I CAN statement is I can solve subtraction word problems. I then explain that we are going to be telling problems about marbles rolling away, and that each time a marble rolls away they get to "SMASH IT!" Everyone gleams with glee because this is going to be too fun. I'm smiling too, because it **is** going to be too fun! And it is going to show them exactly what it means to take something away (to subtract something).*

I give the first problem: Marta had 5 marbles (everyone sets up 5 marbles on the 5 frame mat). Three rolled away. Smash it! They all smash the Play-Doh marbles (which are pre-rolled, by the way, for reasons of personal sanity). We discuss how we had 5 and took away 3, and now there are 2 left. We continue this for about 2 or 3 minutes before I ask who wants to tell a problem of their own. They each eagerly take turns and then the timer rings. I quickly close the lesson by asking "What was the math?" and "How did we practice it?" and everyone soon scurries off to their next workstation.

Figure 2.2

Guided Math Problem Solving Lessons	
Concept	In this lesson, students are trying to understand what the different types of problems are. Some students may be working on change unknown problems and other students may be working on part-part-whole problems. The teacher knows the students and can shape the problem to fit the levels that students are at. This is important because problems should be scaffolded. You want students to be able to unpack the problem so that they can reason about what they are looking for. They have a much better chance of finding it if they know what they are looking for.
Procedural	Procedural problems teach students how to do something. How do we add? What are the rules and procedures for doing that? How do we subtract by modeling it on a number line? How can we model subtraction with a drawing? How do we show it with numbers?
Strategic	Strategic lessons are about students using different strategies to solve problems. Students should be familiar with a variety of strategies and know when and how to use them when problem solving.
Reasoning	Reasoning problems involve students thinking about, justifying, explaining and challenging the thinking of others and defending their own thinking,

Students should spend some time in guided math groups practicing problem solving (see Figure 2.2). These lessons are much more focused and intense and are differentiated toward the needs of the students in the group. These lessons could be concept lessons, procedural lessons, strategy lessons or reasoning lessons.

Problem Solving in Math Workstations

Scenario: Four students are in the problem-solving station. Kelly and Mary have decided to play the word problem sort game. The I CAN statement for this game is I can think about and decide if it is an addition or a subtraction word problem. They are reading the problem and then deciding and sorting it into either an addition or a subtraction column. Mike and David have decided to play the word problem game. The I CAN statement for this game is I can read and solve word problems with answers to 10. In this game they pick a word problem and read it with their partner. They take turns, although they can read it and discuss it together. Then whoever's turn it is has to solve the problem using either tools or templates from their toolkit. If they get the problem correct, they get to keep the card. If they get it incorrect, it goes to the bottom of the pile. Whoever has the most cards by the end of the game wins.

The Problem Solving Math Workstation should be a permanent workstation throughout the year. It should be leveled. Students should be assessed at the beginning of the year to see where they are at and then continue on from there when working in the workstations. Throughout the year, students progress through the problem types at their own speed. There are also a variety of activities that should take place at the workstations.

The table below shows different ways to have students work on problem solving to build mathematical proficiency (see Figure 2.3).

Figure 2.3

Math Workstation Problem Solving Activities	
Concept	In these activities students will work on the different problem types. These activities build the concept of addition, subtraction, part-part-whole and compare problems. These activities include sorting and solving problem types. **Example Activity: I can read and find the missing part in a word problem.** Read the problem. Sort it into a compare looking for the smaller part or compare looking for the bigger part. Matt had 5 marbles. His brother had 2 more than he did. How many did his brother have? / Sort the compare problems. Looking for — Bigger part / Smaller part / Matt had 5 marbles. His brother had 2 fewer than he did. How many did his brother have?
Procedural	These activities provide practice for the procedural fluency element. The emphasis is on the students doing the math correctly and on the procedures of using different models to explain their thinking. **Example Activity: I can model word problems.** Read the problem and draw a bar diagram to solve. Dan had 5 marbles. His brother had 7. How many did they have altogether? / Read the problem and use a number line to solve. Kate jumped 12 inches. Then she jumped 9 more. How far did she jump in total?
Strategic	In these activities students focus on solving one way and checking another. The strategic lessons are about students using different strategies to solve problems. Students should be familiar with a variety of strategies and know when and how to use them when problem solving. **Example Activity: I can solve word problems one way and check another.** Marta had 5 rings. She got 2 more. How many rings does she have now? Solve 1 way: Check another: Answer: / Jamal had 5 marbles. He got some more and now he has 10. How many more did he get? Solve with the 10 frame: Check another way: 1 2 3 4 5 6 7 8 9 10 Answer:
Reasoning (part of reasoning is decontextualizing—going from numbers to words)	Students have to reason about the word problems. **Example Activity: I can write word problems.** The answer is 5 marbles. What is the question? / The answer is 5 marbles. It was a subtraction problem. What is the question?

Key Points

- Daily Practice
- Whole Group
- Process:
  - Visualize
  - Summarize
  - Make a plan
  - Solve one way
  - Check another
  - Double-double-check
  - Explain
- Guided Math Group
- Math Workstations
- Templates

Summary

Problem solving should be done throughout the workshop from routines, through guided math lessons and in math workstations. A daily whole-group routine helps to teach the practice/process of problem solving. It builds the "habit of mind" and "way of being" as a problem solver. It routinizes the process so that students focus on the type of problem, the plan, the process of solving the problem with models and strategies and, finally, the double-checking.

The small group lesson allows the teacher to differentiate problem solving to meet the needs of the learners. There are 4 categories of addition and subtraction problems and 2 categories of multi-step (including two-step and then multi-step). Since there are different levels of these problems, it is important for teachers to meet the individual needs of students because some might be working on level 4 problems and others might be working on level 7 problems.

Math workstation allows the students to practice at their level with scaffolds. The students get to work in their zone of proximal development (Vygotsky, 1978), and they get practice until they master that level and then move to the next. In workstations, students also get to work with partners and sometimes in a group to think about problems and listen to the reasoning of others to decide if it makes sense or not. This type of work allows students to widen their repertoire for problem solving.

Reflection Questions

1. Do you integrate problem solving throughout your math period?
2. Do you do problem solving daily with an emphasis on building the *habit of mind* rather than on *getting the answer*?
3. Do you pull small groups in order to work with students in their zone of proximal development?
4. Do you give students the opportunity to build their skills in differentiated, leveled workstations?
5. What is your big takeaway from this chapter? What one thing in your teaching will you start or expand?

References

Daro, P. Beyond Answer Getting. Retrieved on January 17, 2016 from https://vimeo.com/79916037

Gojak, L. (2011). *What's your math problem? Getting to the heart of teaching problem solving.* Huntington Beach, CA: Shell Education.

National Council of Teachers of Mathematics (NCTM). (2000). *Principles and standards for school mathematics.* Reston, VA: NCTM. Retrieved August 4, 2015 from http://mrflip.com/teach/resources/NCTM/chapter3/numb.htm.

National Governors Association Center for Best Practices and Council of Chief State School Officers (NGA Center). (2010). *Common core state standards for mathematics.* Washington, DC: Authors.

Vygotsky, L. S. (1978). *Mind in society: The development of higher psychological processes.* Cambridge, MA: Harvard University Press.

3

The Basic Framework

Cognitively Guided Instruction (CGI)—Starting with Structure

All state standards use some type of schema-based framework for story problems. A schema is a way of organizing word problems by type. There has been a great deal of research on the effectiveness of schema-based word problems in teaching and learning (Willis and Fuson, 1988; Jitendra and Hoff, 1996; Fuchs et al., 2004; Griffin and Jitendra, 2009).

One of the most informative professional development books to teach schema-based problem solving is *Children's Mathematics: Cognitively Guided Instruction* (Carpenter et al., 2014). The research from the book frames problem solving around getting students to understand the different problems conceptually, so that they can reason, use efficient strategies and have procedural fluency.

Furthermore, the research makes the case that the key word method should be avoided! Students should learn to understand the problem types and what they are actually discussing rather than "key word" tricks. The thing about key words is that they only work with simplistic problems, so as students do more sophisticated work with word problems, the key words do not serve them well. The key words may actually lead them in the wrong direction, often encouraging the wrong operation. For example, consider this problem: John has 2 apples. Kate has 3 more than he does. How many do they have altogether? Many students just add 2 and 3 instead of unpacking the problem. Here is another example: Sue has 10 marbles. She has 2 times as many marbles as Lucy. How many marbles does Lucy have? Oftentimes, students just multiply because they see the word times, instead of reading and understanding the problem.

Introduction to the Types of Problems

There are 4 general categories for addition and subtraction problems (see Figure 3.1). After the students have mastered these problems, they begin to work on two-step and multi-step problems.

Figure 3.1

Join/Separate	Result Unknown	Change Unknown	Start Unknown
Join	Marta had 5 marbles. She got 2 more. How many does she have now? 5 + 2 = ?	Marta had 5 marbles. She got some more. Now she has 7. How many did she get? 5 + ? = 7 7 − 5 = ?	Marta had some marbles. She got 2 more. Now she has 5. How many did she have in the beginning? ? + 2 = 5
Separate	Joe had 10 marbles. He gave 2 to his brother. How many does he have left? 10 − 2 = ?	Joe had 10 marbles. He gave some to his friends. Now he has 5 left. How many did he give away? 10 − ? = 5	Joe had some marbles. He gave 3 away. Now he has 7. How many did he have in the beginning? ? − 3 = 7
Part-Part-Whole	**Whole Unknown**	**Both Addends Unknown**	**Part Unknown**
	Jamal had 3 big marbles and 4 small marbles. How many did he have altogether? 3 + 4 = ?	Jamal had 7 marbles. Some were big and some were small. How many of each could he have? 7 + 0; 6 + 1; 5 + 2; 4 + 3; 3 + 4; 2 + 5; 1 + 6; 0 + 7	Jamal had 7 marbles. 3 were big. The rest were small. How many were small? 7 − 3 = ? 3 + ? = 7
Compare	**Difference** **Easy Version**	**Bigger Part Unknown** **Easy Version**	**Smaller Part Unknown** **Easy Version**
	Grace had 7 rings. Lucy had 4. How many more rings did Grace have than Lucy? 7 − 4 = ? 4 + ? = 7	Lucy had 4 rings. Grace had 3 more than she did. How many did Grace have? 4 + 3 = ?	Grace had 7 rings. Lucy had 3 fewer than she did. How many did Lucy have? 7 − 3 = ?
Compare	**Difference** **Harder Version**	**Bigger Part Unknown** **Harder Version**	**Smaller Part Unknown** **Harder Version**
	Grace had 4 rings. Lucy had 7. How many fewer rings did Grace have than Lucy? 7 − 4 = ? 4 + ? = 7	Lucy had 4 rings. She had 3 fewer than Grace. How many did Grace have? 4 + 3 = ?	Grace had 7 rings. She had 3 more than Lucy. How many did Lucy have? 7 − 3 = ?

Two-Step Problems and More

After students have mastered solving one-step problems, they start working on two-step problems and then multi-step problems. There is still a leveled hierarchy that is often neglected. This is highly detrimental to student learning because two-step and multi-step problems are simply one-step problems with two or more parts. It is important to remember to scaffold levels of difficulty so that the cognitive load is balanced. Don't give hard problems with hard numbers to start with because then students become cognitively overloaded.

Give hard problem types with easy numbers so that students can focus on the problem. Once they know how to solve the problem, then give harder numbers. Often the problem is that students don't fully understand one of the parts. So it is crucial that students understand the one-step problems before they go on to others. This must be assessed and addressed on an ongoing basis.

How Do We Teach This?

These are a lot of different problem types. The research states that teachers should teach the types explicitly to the students and that the students should be able to name the type of problem they are solving. But the terminology isn't that important. It is the concept that teachers should emphasize and that students should know. Students need to know that they are putting stuff together or taking it apart. They should understand whether or not they are looking for the amount in each group or if they are looking for the amount of groups. They should think about whether this is a one-step, two-step or multi-step problem. This just helps students to unpack a problem and make a plan for solving it. Because if students know what they are looking for, then they are much more likely to find it!

Word Problems in the 21st Century

Students can either do some Web-based activities in the word problem workstation or in the digital workstation (see Figure 3.2). There are some great sites for students to practice word problems. Math Playground has Thinking Blocks, where students can work through a series of models for tape diagramming problems based on the operation. This is a fantastic site (Math Playground: www.mathplayground.com/ThinkingBlocks/thinking_blocks_start).

Greg Tang has also recently built a whole world of word problem activities where students can pick the word problem by type and even get hints about how to set up the problem with tape diagrams. If the students do one problem at a time, they can get the hints and the answers. This is how I recommend that they practice it. There is also an option to generate several word problems at a time, but these just give the word

Figure 3.2

Picture Books/Stories	Use picture books as a launch into different problem contexts. There is a great book called *Tall Tale Math* by Betsy Franco specifically for grades 3–5 that mathematizes tall tales.
Paper and Virtual Tools	Use a variety of physical and virtual manipulatives to solve problems. For virtual manipulatives, see: http://nlvm.usu.edu/ www.glencoe.com/sites/common_assets/mathematics/ebook_assets/vmf/VMF-Interface.html
Word Problem Websites	www.mathplayground.com/thinkingblocks.html https://learnzillion.com/p/ http://gregtangmath.com/materials www.mathplayground.com/wp_videos.html www.mathplayground.com/ThinkingBlocks/thinking_blocks_start.html
Online Resources	www.illustrativemathematics.org/ www.insidemathematics.org/ https://sddial.k12.sd.us/esa/grants/sdcounts/

problems without all of the scaffolding. (See the Greg Tang Word Problem Generator: http://gregtangmath.com/wordproblems.)

Key Points

- CGI provides a framework for teaching word problems (Carpenter et al., 2014).
- The emphasis should be on the problem types and structure rather than on key words.
- There are four major categories for addition and subtraction.
- There are levels for two-step problems.
- There are different types of multi-step problems.
- There are many 21st-century tools to teach word problems.

Summary

Schema-based problem solving is a framework that is used to teach word problems (Carpenter et al., 2014). Many educators did not learn word problems from this framework and need to take the time to understand it so that they can better teach them. Students should learn to think about the structure and type of problem so they can set it up accordingly. Students should also focus on how many steps the problem involves so that they can prepare for that in the planning and double-check all the parts in the end. There are many great resources to teach problem solving and to practice problems that are free and valuable these days.

Reflection Questions

1. Do you presently teach with the word problem types in mind?
2. Do you presently get students to think about the steps involved in the word problem? If so, how do you currently do it? If not, how might this help?
3. Do you use technology to teach and practice word problems?
4. What are your biggest takeaways from this chapter?

References

Carpenter, T. P., Fennema, E., Franke, M. L., Levi, L., and Empson, S. B. (2014). *Children's mathematics: Cognitively guided instruction* (2nd ed.). Portsmouth, NH: Heinemann.

Fuchs, L. S., Fuchs, D., Finelli, R., Courey, S. J., and Hamlett, C. L. (2004). Expanding schema-based transfer instruction to help third graders solve real-life mathematical problems. *American Educational Research Journal*, 41(2), 419–445.

Griffin, C. C., and Jitendra, A. K. (2009). Word problem-solving instruction in inclusive third-grade classrooms. *The Journal of Educational Research*, 102(3), 187–201.

Jitendra, A., and Hoff, K. (1996). The effects of schema-based instruction on mathematical word problem solving performance of students with learning disabilities. *Journal of Learning Disabilities*, 29(3), 422–431.

Willis, G. B, and Fuson, K. C. (1988). Teaching children to use schematic drawings to solve addition and subtraction word problems. *Journal of Educational Psychology*, 80(2), 192–201.

Part II

A Deeper Dive

4

Add To Problems

Add To Problem Types

Add to problems are all about adding. There are three types (see Figure 4.1). The first type of *add to* problem is where the result is unknown (see Figures 4.2 through 4.11). For example: *The cafeteria had 57 students in it. Then, 29 more students came. How many people are in the cafeteria now?* In this problem, the result is unknown. Teachers tend to tell these types of problems. They are basic and straightforward. The teacher should start with concrete items, then proceed to drawing out the story, then to diagramming the story and, finally, to using equations to represent the story. The "results unknown" problem is the easiest type of story problem to solve.

The second kind of *add to* problem is the *change unknown* problem. For example: *The toy store had 50 marbles. It got some more. Now the toy store has 72 marbles. How many marbles did the toy store get?* Another example: *Maria had 5 rings. She got some more for her birthday. Now she has 15 rings. How many did she get for her birthday?* In this type of problem, the students are looking for the change (see Figures 4.12 through 4.21). They know the start and they know the end, but they don't know the *change*.

The third type of *add to* problem is a *start unknown* problem. For example: *The toy store had some marbles. They got 14 more on Wednesday. Now they have 20 marbles. How many did they have in the beginning?* In this type of problem, the students are looking for the start (see Figures 4.22 through 4.29). This is the hardest type of *add to* problem to solve, and it takes a great deal of modeling.

Figure 4.1

Problem Types	Result Unknown	Change Unknown	Start Unknown
Join/Adding to	Marco had 5 marbles. His brother gave him 5 more. How many does he have now?	Marco had 5 marbles. His brother gave him some more. Now he has 10. How many did his brother give him?	Marco had some marbles. His brother gave him 5 more. Now he has 10. How many did he have in the beginning?
Bar Diagram Modeling Problem	? | 5 | 5 |	10 | 5 | ? |	10 | ? | 5 |
What are we looking for? Where is *X*?	Both addends are known. We are looking for the total amount. The result is the unknown. In other words, we know what we started with and we know the change, we are looking for the end.	The first addend is known. The result is also known. We are looking for the change. The change is unknown. In other words, we know what happened at the start and we know what happened at the end. We are looking for the change. We need to find out what happened in the middle.	The second addend is known. The result is known. We are looking for the start. The start is unknown. In other words, we know the change and we know the end but we don't know what happened at the beginning.
Algebraic Sentence	5 + 5 = ?	5 + ? = 10 10 – 5 = ?	x + 5 = 10
Strategies to Solve	Add/ Count up	Count up/Subtract	Count up/Subtract
Answer	He has 10 marbles now.	He gave him 5 marbles.	He had 5 marbles in the beginning.

Concrete Models

Number Frames

Problem: Carlos had 2 marbles. He got 2 more. How many does he have
             now?
Strategy: Count on

Figure 4.2

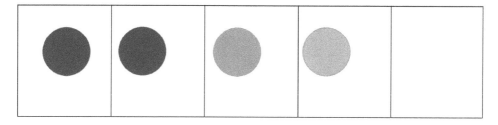

Problem: Anna had 4 marbles. She got 6 more. How many does she have
             now?
Strategy: Ten friends

Figure 4.3

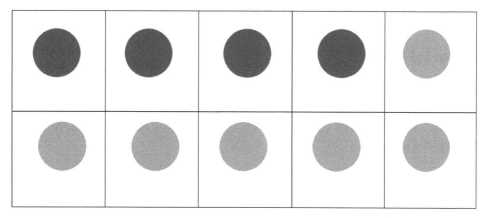

Problem: Jamal had 4 marbles. He got 8 more. How many does he have now?
Strategy: Bridge 10

Figure 4.4

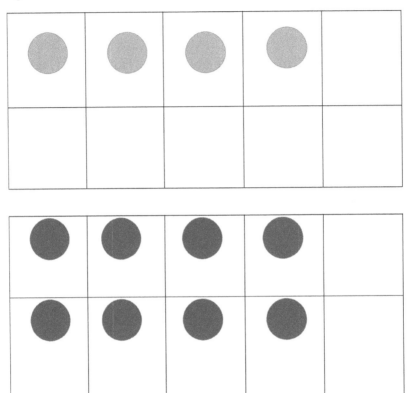

Pictorial Models

Drawings and Sketches

Problem: Missy had 4 dolls. She got 3 more. How many does she have now?
Strategy: Count on

Figure 4.5

Abstract Models

Number Grids

Problem: Jake had 12 marbles. He got 5 more. How many does he have
now?
Strategy: Count on

Figure 4.6

1	2	3	4	5	6	7	8	9	10
11	12	13	14	15	16	17	18	19	20

Problem: Maria had 22 marbles. She got 15 more. How many does she
have now?
Strategy: Use number grid slides. Slide down 10 and over 5. Also, you
could add tens and then add ones.

Figure 4.7

1	2	3	4	5	6	7	8	9	10
11	12	13	14	15	16	17	18	19	20
21	22	23	24	25	26	27	28	29	30
31	32	33	34	35	36	37	38	39	40
41	42	43	44	45	46	47	48	49	50

Problem: Lisa had 57 marbles. She got 22 more. How many does she have
now?
Strategy: Use number grid slides. Slide down 20 and over 2. Also, you
could add tens and then add ones.

Figure 4.8

1	2	3	4	5	6	7	8	9	10
11	12	13	14	15	16	17	18	19	20
21	22	23	24	25	26	27	28	29	30
31	32	33	34	35	36	37	38	39	40
41	42	43	44	45	46	47	48	49	50
51	52	53	54	55	56	57	58	59	60
61	62	63	64	65	66	67	68	69	70
71	72	73	74	75	76	77	78	79	80
81	82	83	84	85	86	87	88	89	90
91	92	93	94	95	96	97	98	99	100

Number Lines

Problem: Lisa had 5 marbles. She got 2 more. How many does she have now?
Strategy: Count on

Figure 4.9

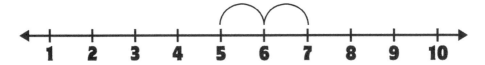

Problem: Tim had 8 marbles. He got 4 more. How many does he have now?
Strategy: Bridge 10 . . . count to 10 and then on.

Figure 4.10

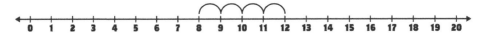

Problem: Greg had 50 marbles. He got 20 more. How many does he have now?
Strategy: Jumping tens

Figure 4.11

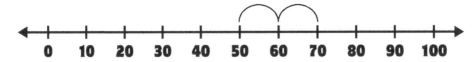

Problem: Marline had 34 marbles. She got 27 more. How many does she have now?
Strategy: Count up to a friendly number and then on from there.

Figure 4.12

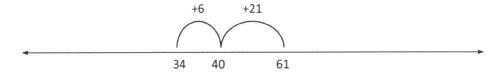

Add to Change Unknown Problems

Concrete Models

Number Frames

Problem: Carlos had 2 marbles. He got some more. Now he has 5 marbles. How many did he get?
Strategy: Count up or subtract

Figure 4.13

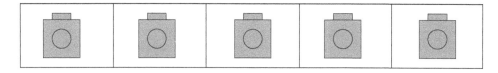

Problem: Anna had 4 marbles. She got some more. Now she has 10. How many did she get?
Strategy: Ten friends or count up or subtract

Figure 4.14

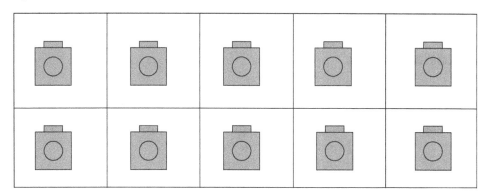

Problem: Jamal had 10 cubes. He got some more. Now he has 18 cubes. How many did he get?

Strategy: Adding to tens or count up or subtract

Figure 4.15

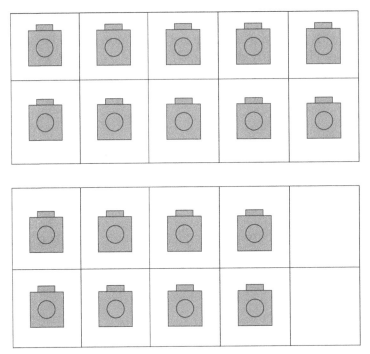

Pictorial Models

Drawings and Sketches

Problem: Missy had 25 marbles. She got some more. Now she has 50 marbles. How many did she get?

Strategy: Doubles or count tens and ones

Figure 4.16

Abstract Models

Number Grids

Problem: Jake had 12 marbles. He got some more. Now he has 17. How
many did he get?
Strategy: Add 10 and ones

Figure 4.17

1	2	3	4	5	6	7	8	9	10
11	12	13	14	15	16	17	18	19	20

Problem: Maria had 22 marbles. She got some more. Now she has 37.
How many did she get?
Strategy: Slide down 10 and over 5 to 37.

Figure 4.18

1	2	3	4	5	6	7	8	9	10
11	12	13	14	15	16	17	18	19	20
21	22	23	24	25	26	27	28	29	30
31	32	33	34	35	36	37	38	39	40
41	42	43	44	45	46	47	48	49	50

Problem: Lisa had 57 marbles. She got some more. Now she has 70 marbles. How many did she get?
Strategy: Slide down to 67 and over 3.

Figure 4.19

1	2	3	4	5	6	7	8	9	10
11	12	13	14	15	16	17	18	19	20
21	22	23	24	25	26	27	28	29	30
31	32	33	34	35	36	37	38	39	40
41	42	43	44	45	46	47	48	49	50
51	52	53	54	55	56	57	58	59	60
61	62	63	64	65	66	67	68	69	70
71	72	73	74	75	76	77	78	79	80
81	82	83	84	85	86	87	88	89	90
91	92	93	94	95	96	97	98	99	100

Number Lines

Problem: Lisa had 5 marbles. She got some more. Now she has 10. How many did she get?

Strategy: Ten friends

Figure 4.20

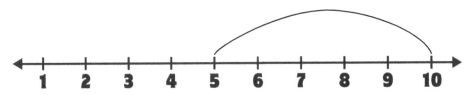

Problem: Tim had 8 marbles. He got some more. Now he has 12 marbles. How many did he get?

Strategy: Bridge 10 or count up

Figure 4.21

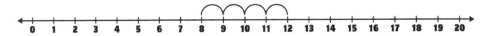

Problem: Greg had 50 marbles. He got some more. Now he has 100. How many did he get?

Strategy: 100 friends or count up

Figure 4.22

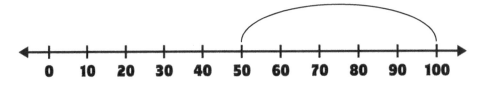

Open Number Lines

Problem: Marline had 34 marbles. She got some more. Now she has 61.
How many did she get?

Strategy: Jump to a friendly number and then jump on

Figure 4.23

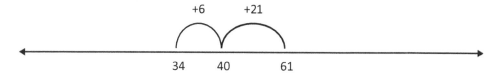

Concrete Models

Number Frames

Problem: Carlos had some marbles. He got 2 more. Now he has 5 marbles. How many did he have in the beginning?

Strategy: Count up

Figure 4.24

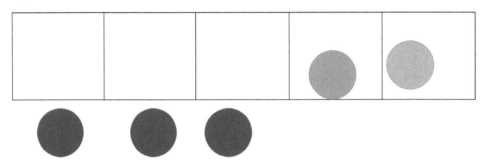

Problem: Anna had some marbles. She got 6 more. Now she has 10 marbles. How many did she have in the beginning?

Strategy: Ten friends

Figure 4.25

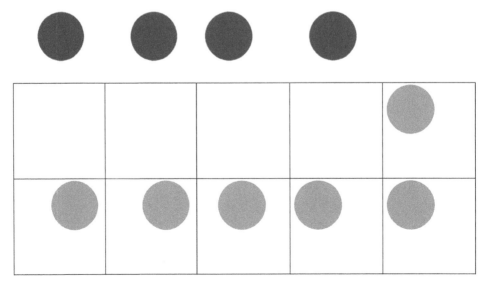

Pictorial Models

Drawings and Sketches

Problem: There were some kids in the house. 3 more came. Now there are 6 kids. How many kids were there to start with?

Strategy: Doubles facts or count up or subtract

Figure 4.26

Abstract Models

Number Grids

Problem: Jake had some marbles. He got 5 more. Now he has 17. How many did he have in the beginning?

Strategy: Subtract 5 from 17

Figure 4.27

1	2	3	4	5	6	7	8	9	10
11	12	13	14	15	16	17	18	19	20

Problem: Maria had some marbles. She got 15 more. Now she has 40 marbles. How many did she have in the beginning?

Strategy: Think 15 and what number make 40, or subtract.

Figure 4.28

1	2	3	4	5	6	7	8	9	10
11	12	13	14	15	16	17	18	19	20
21	22	23	24	25	26	27	28	29	30
31	32	33	34	35	36	37	38	39	40
41	42	43	44	45	46	47	48	49	50

Problem: Lisa had some marbles. She got 22 more. Now she has 50. How many did she have in the beginning?

Strategy: Think 22 plus what number makes 50, or subtract.

Figure 4.29

1	2	3	4	5	6	7	8	9	10
11	12	13	14	15	16	17	18	19	20
21	22	23	24	25	26	27	28	29	30
31	32	33	34	35	36	37	38	39	40
41	42	43	44	45	46	47	48	49	50
51	52	53	54	55	56	57	58	59	60
61	62	63	64	65	66	67	68	69	70
71	72	73	74	75	76	77	78	79	80
81	82	83	84	85	86	87	88	89	90
91	92	93	94	95	96	97	98	99	100

Number Lines

Problem: Lisa had some marbles. She got 2 more. Now she has 7 marbles. How many did she have in the beginning?

Strategy: Think 2 plus what number makes 7, or subtract

Figure 4.30

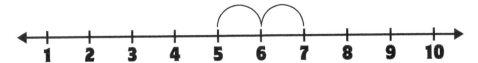

Problem: Tim had some marbles. He got 4 more. Now he has 12 marbles. How many did he have in the beginning?

Strategy: Think 4 and what number makes 12, or subtract.

Figure 4.31

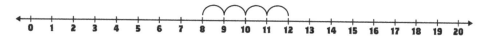

Problem: Greg had some marbles. He got 20 more. Now he has 70 marbles. How many did he have in the beginning?

Strategy: Think 20 and what number makes 50, or subtract.

Figure 4.32

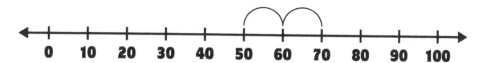

Assessment

When assessing word problems, it is important to check many aspects. Notice that the following example checks all of the versions (that are taught at a specific grade). Check to see if the students can solve one way and check their work by another. Check to see if students can use a variety of models and strategies. Make sure that they can explain what they did. See if they can write the different types of problems as well as solve them. Notice there are 2 bonus questions where students are asked to match equations with the story and then the story with the equation. This is very important because it gives us insight into whether students can reason about numbers or not.

Figure 4.33

1. Mary had 8 rings. She got 10 more. How many rings does Mary have now?
   A. Write an equation showing the missing part.

   B. Model your thinking with a sketch.

   C. Model your thinking with a double 10 frame.

   D. Answer: _____

2. Mark had 8 toy cars. He got some more. Now he has 10. How many did he get?

   A. Model your thinking.

   B. Check your answer a different way.

   C. Answer: _____

3. Kelli had some dolls. She got 2 more. Now she has 5 dolls. How many did she have in the beginning?
   A. Model your thinking.

   B. Check your answer a different way.

   C. Answer: _____

   D. Explain what you did.

4. Joe had 8 marbles. He got some more. Now he has 12. How many did he get?

   Which number sentences can you use to answer this problem?

   A. $8 + 12 =$ _____
   B. $8 +$ ___ $= 12$
   C. None of the above

5. $2 + 5 = 7$

   Which story matches this equation?

   A. Mike had 2 marbles and he got 5 more.
   B. Mike had 7 marbles and he gave away 2.
   C. None of the above

6. The answer is 10 marbles. What is the question?

   Write a story where the answer is 10 marbles.

   A. Write the story
   B. Model your story
   C. Number sentence

Key Points

- CGI provides a framework for teaching word problems (Carpenter et al., 2014).
- The emphasis should be on the problem types and structure rather than on keywords.
- There are 3 types of addition problems.
  - The easiest type of addition problem is the *add to result unknown*.
  - A more challenging version is the *add to change unknown*.
  - The most challenging type of addition problem is the *add to start unknown*.
- Students should use and be able to describe a variety of models when solving problems.
- Students should use and be able to describe a variety of strategies when solving problems.

Summary

Add to word problems are the first type of problems students learn. They start learning them in kindergarten and continue adding the problem types from this category through 1st and 2nd grade. Students find the *change unknown* and the *start unknown* problems very challenging. Although the *change unknown* problems are often started in first grade, it is often advised that teachers wait to teach the *start unknown* until the other levels of word problems have been mastered. *Start unknown* problems are very challenging. All problems should be taught using a variety of models and strategies so that students can explain how they are thinking about the problem and what they are doing with the numbers.

Reflection Questions

1. How do you approach the addition problem types?
2. How do you scaffold learning these types with different models and strategies?
3. Do you use technology to teach and practice word problems?
4. What are your biggest takeaways from this chapter?

Reference

Carpenter, T. P., Fennema, E., Franke, M. L., Levi, L., and Empson, S. B. (2014). *Children's mathematics: Cognitively guided instruction* (2nd ed.). Portsmouth, NH: Heinemann.

5

Take From Problems

Take From Problems

Take from problems are all about subtracting (see Figure 5.1). There are three types (see Figure 5.2 through Figure 5.10). The first type is *take from* problems where the result is unknown. For example: *The bookstore had 42 magazines. Then they sold 8. How many do they have now?* Another example: *John had $20. He spent $3. How much does he have left?* In this problem, the result is unknown. Teachers often tell these types of problems. They are basic and straightforward.

The second kind of *take from* problem is the *change unknown* problem. For example: *The toy store had 50 toy cars. They sold some. They have 19 left. How many did they sell?* Another example: *The bakery made 12 cupcakes. They sold some of them. They have 7 left. How many did they sell?* In this type of problem, the students are looking for the change (see Figures 5.11 through 5.20). They know the start and they know the end, but they don't know the *change*.

The third type of *take from* problem is a *start unknown* problem. For example: *Jenny had some money. She gave John $4. Now she has $6 left. How much money did she have in the beginning?* In this type of problem, the students are looking for the start (see Figures 5.21 through 5.30). This is the hardest type of *take from* problem to solve and it takes a great deal of modeling.

Figure 5.1

Problem Types	Result Unknown	Change Unknown	Start Unknown
Separate/ Take From	Marco had 10 marbles. He gave his brother 4. How many does he have left?	Marco had 10 marbles. He gave some away. Now he has 5 left. How many did he give away?	Marco had some marbles. He gave 2 away and now he has 5 left. How many did he have to start with?
Bar Diagram Modeling Problem	10 — [4 | ?]	10 — [? | 5]	? — [2 | 5]
What are we looking for? Where is *X*?	In this story we know the beginning and what happened in the middle. The mystery is what happened at the end. The result is unknown.	In this story we know the beginning and the end. The mystery is what happened in the middle. The change is unknown.	In this story we know what happened in the middle and what happened at the end. The mystery is how did it start? The start is unknown.
Algebraic Sentence	$10 - 4 = ?$	$10 - ? = 5$ $5 + x = 10$	$? - 2 = 5$ $2 + 5 = ?$
Strategies to Solve	Subtract	Subtract or count up	Count up/Subtract
Answer	$10 - 4 = 6$ He had 6 marbles left.	$10 - 5 = 5$ $5 + 5 = 10$ He gave away 5 marbles.	$7 - 2 = 5$ $2 + 5 = 7$ He had 7 marbles in the beginning.

Take From Result Unknown

Concrete Models

Number Frames

Problem: Carlos had 5 marbles. He gave 2 away. How many does he have now?
Strategy: Put 5 markers on a template and then take 2 away.

Figure 5.2

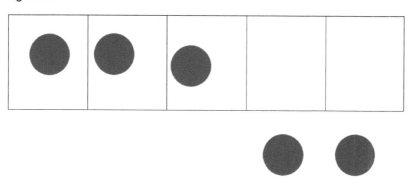

Problem: Anna had 9 marbles. She gave 6 away. How many does she have now?
Strategy: Put 9 markers on a template and then take 6 away.

Figure 5.3

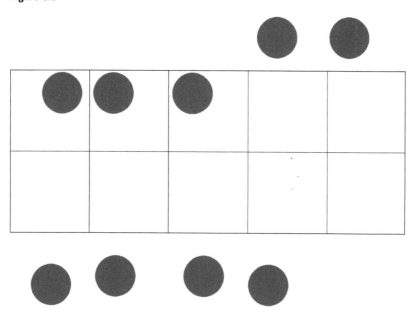

Problem: Jamal had 14 marbles. He gave 8 away. How many does he have now?

Strategy: Bridge 10/partial differences (subtract 4 from 14 to get to 10 and then 4 more to get to 6).

Figure 5.4

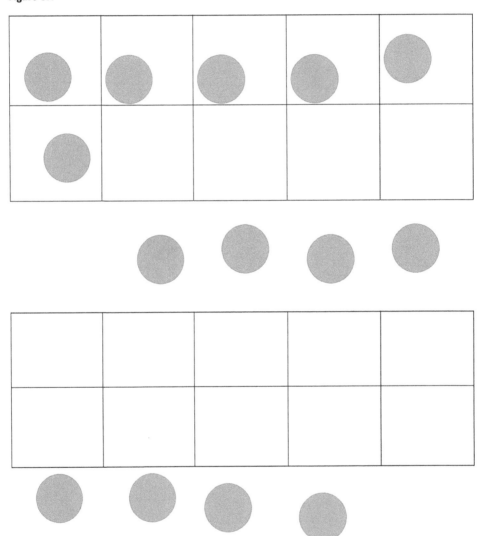

Pictorial Models

Drawings and Sketches

Problem: Missy had 10 dolls. She gave 4 away. How many does she have now?

Strategy: Ten friends or draw 10 dolls and cross out 4.

Figure 5.5

Abstract Models

Number Grids

Problem: Maria had 22 marbles. She gave 8 away. How many does she have now?

Strategy: Count back 10 and then add 2 more back because we were only supposed to take 8 away.

Figure 5.6

1	2	3	4	5	6	7	8	9	10
11	12	13	14	15	16	17	18	19	20
21	22	23	24	25	26	27	28	29	30
31	32	33	34	35	36	37	38	39	40
41	42	43	44	45	46	47	48	49	50

Problem: Lisa had 57 marbles. She gave away 39. How many does she have now?

Strategy: Jump back 40 and then add 1 back because we were only supposed to take away 39.

Figure 5.7

1	2	3	4	5	6	7	8	9	10
11	12	13	14	15	16	17	18	19	20
21	22	23	24	25	26	27	28	29	30
31	32	33	34	35	36	37	38	39	40
41	42	43	44	45	46	47	48	49	50
51	52	53	54	55	56	57	58	59	60
61	62	63	64	65	66	67	68	69	70
71	72	73	74	75	76	77	78	79	80
81	82	83	84	85	86	87	88	89	90
91	92	93	94	95	96	97	98	99	100

Number Lines

Problem: Lisa had 7 marbles. She gave 2 away. How many does she have now?

Strategy: Use the number line. Start at 7 and jump back 2.

Figure 5.8

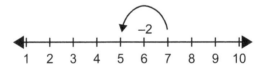

Problem: Tammy had 8 marbles. She gave 4 away. How many does she
have now?
Strategy: Half fact or count up or count back

Figure 5.9

Problem: Greg had 50 marbles. He gave 20 away. How many does he
have now?
Strategy: Subtracting tens

Figure 5.10

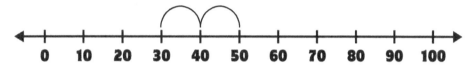

Open Number Lines

Problem: Marline had 61 marbles. She gave 27 away. How many does she
have now?
Strategy: Start at 61. Jump back 30 and then add 3.

Figure 5.11

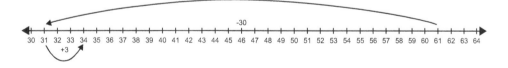

Take From Change Unknown

Concrete Models

Number Frames

Problem: The store had 5 teddy bears. They sold some. Now there are 3 left. How many did they sell?

Strategy: Put 5 markers on a template and then take 2 away.

Figure 5.12

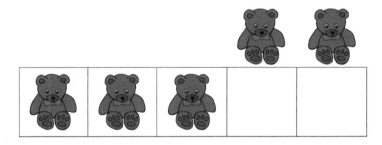

Problem: Mimi had 7 teddy bears. She gave some to her sister. Now she has 4 left. How many did she give to her sister?

Strategy: Put 7 markers on a template and then take away enough so that only 4 are left.

Figure 5.13

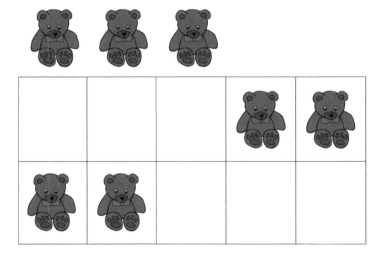

Problem: Jamal had 14 marbles. He gave some away. Now he has 7 left. How many did he give away?

Strategy: Half facts

Figure 5.14

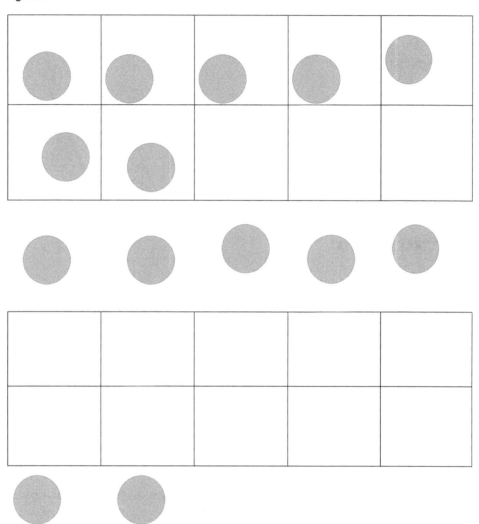

Pictorial Models

Drawings and Sketches

Problem: Missy had 6 dolls. She gave some away. She has 4 left. How many did she give away?

Strategy: Draw 6 dolls and cross out 2.

Figure 5.15

Abstract Models

Number Grids

Problem: Jake had 12 marbles. He gave some away. Now he has 11 marbles. How many did he give away?

Strategy: Differences of 1

Figure 5.16

1	2	3	4	5	6	7	8	9	10
11 ◄— 12		13	14	15	16	17	18	19	20

Problem: Maria had 22 marbles. She gave some away. Now she has 10 left. How many did she give away?

Strategy: Count back or count up

Figure 5.17

1	2	3	4	5	6	7	8	9	10 ◄—
11 ◄— 12 ▲		13	14	15	16	17	18	19	20
21	22	23	24	25	26	27	28	29	30
31	32	33	34	35	36	37	38	39	40
41	42	43	44	45	46	47	48	49	50

Problem: Lisa had 82 marbles. She gave some away. Now she has 50 left. How many did she give away?

Strategy: Count back or count up

Figure 5.18

1	2	3	4	5	6	7	8	9	10
11	12	13	14	15	16	17	18	19	20
21	22	23	24	25	26	27	28	29	30
31	32	33	34	35	36	37	38	39	40
41	42	43	44	45	46	47	48	49	50 ←
51 ←	52 ↑	53	54	55	56	57	58	59	60
61	62	63	64	65	66	67	68	69	70
71	72	73	74	75	76	77	78	79	80
81	82	83	84	85	86	87	88	89	90
91	92	93	94	95	96	97	98	99	100

Number Lines

Problem: Lisa had 7 marbles. She gave some away. Now she has 5 left. How many did she give away?

Strategy: Use the number line. Start at 7 and jump back 2.

Figure 5.19

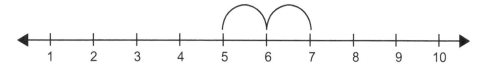

Problem: Tammy had 12 marbles. She gave some away. Now she has 8 marbles. How many did she give away?

Strategy: Bridge 10 (start at 12, jump to 10 and then 2 more).

Figure 5.20

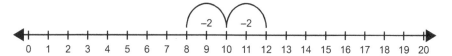

Number Lines to 100

Problem: Greg had 70 marbles. He gave some away. Now he has 50 left.
How many did he give away?
Strategy: Use the number line. Start at 70 and jump back 20.

Figure 5.21

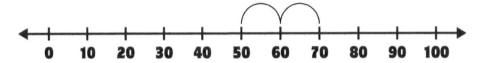

Open Number Lines

Problem: Marline had 90 marbles. She gave some away. Now she has 75
marbles left. How many did she give away?
Strategy: Start at 90 and jump back 10 and 5. Or, count up from 75 to 90.

Figure 5.22

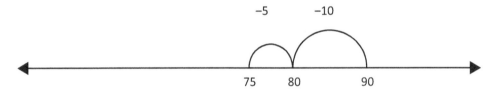

Take From Start Unknown

Concrete Models

Number Frames

Problem: The store had some teddy bears. They sold 2. Now there are 3
left. How many did they have in the beginning?
Strategy: Add 2 and 3.

Figure 5.23

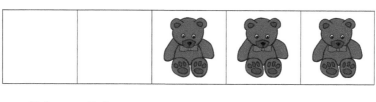

Problem: Mimi had some teddy bears. She gave 3 to her sister. Now she
has 4 left. How many did she have in the beginning?
Strategy: Add 3 and 4.

Figure 5.24

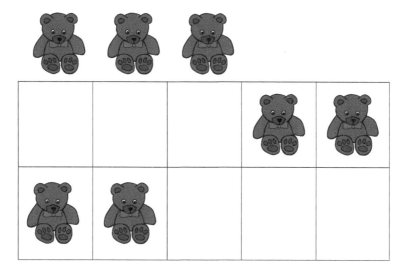

Problem: Jamal had some marbles. He gave 7 away. Now he has 7 left. How many did he have in the beginning?

Strategy: Doubles

Figure 5.25

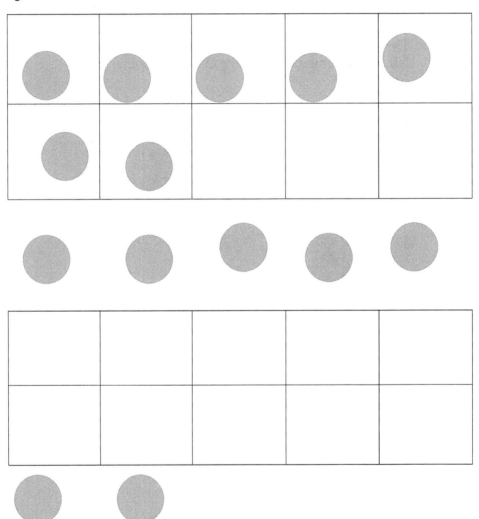

Pictorial Models

Drawings and Sketches

Problem: Missy had some dolls. She gave 4 away. She has 4 left. How
many did she have in the beginning?
Strategy: Draw 8 dolls and cross out 4 or use doubles facts.

Figure 5.26

Abstract Models

Number Grids

Problem: Jake had some marbles. He gave 10 away. Now he has 4 marbles. How many did he have in the beginning?
Strategy: Add 10 and 4.

Figure 5.27

1	2	3	4	5	6	7	8	9	10
11	12	13	14	15	16	17	18	19	20

Problem: Maria had some marbles. She gave 10 away. Now she has 10
left. How many did have in the beginning?
Strategy: Doubles facts

Figure 5.28

1	2	3	4	5	6	7	8	9	10
11	12	13	14	15	16	17	18	19	20
21	22	23	24	25	26	27	28	29	30
31	32	33	34	35	36	37	38	39	40
41	42	43	44	45	46	47	48	49	50

Problem: Lisa had some marbles. She gave 20 away. Now she has 50 left. How many did she have in the beginning?

Strategy: Add 20 and 50.

Figure 5.29

1	2	3	4	5	6	7	8	9	10
11	12	13	14	15	16	17	18	19	20
21	22	23	24	25	26	27	28	29	30
31	32	33	34	35	36	37	38	39	40
41	42	43	44	45	46	47	48	49	50
51	52	53	54	55	56	57	58	59	60
61	62	63	64	65	66	67	68	69	70
71	72	73	74	75	76	77	78	79	80
81	82	83	84	85	86	87	88	89	90
91	92	93	94	95	96	97	98	99	100

Number Lines

Problem: Lisa had some marbles. She gave 5 away. Now she has 5 left. How many did she have in the beginning?

Strategy: Doubles facts or add 5 and 5.

Figure 5.30

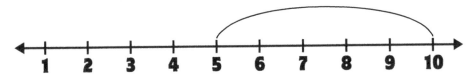

Problem: Tammy had some marbles. She gave 14 away. Now she has 4 marbles. How many did she have in the beginning?

Strategy: Count up 4 from 14.

Figure 5.31

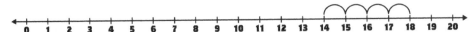

Problem: Greg had some marbles. He gave 50 away. Now he has 50 left. How many did he have in the beginning?
Strategy: Count up or back or use doubles

Figure 5.32

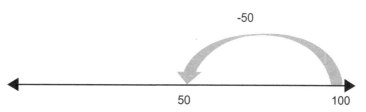

Open Number Lines

Problem: Marline had some marbles. She gave 15 away. Now she has 75 marbles left. How many did she have in the beginning?
Strategy: Count up

Figure 5.33

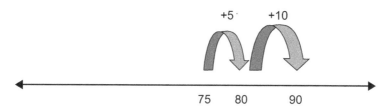

Assessment

When assessing word problems, it is important to check many aspects (see Figure 5.34). Notice that the following example checks both the easy versions and the harder versions. Check to see if the students can solve one way and check by another. Check to see if students can use a variety of models and strategies. Make sure that they can explain what they did. See if they can write the different types of problems as well as solve them.

Figure 5.34

1. Mary had 5 rings. She gave Lucy 2 of them. How many does she have left?
   A. Model your thinking with a sketch.

   B. Model your thinking with a 5 frame.

   C. Answer: _____

2. Mark had 10 toy cars. He got some more. Now he has 14. How many did he get?
   A. Model your thinking.

   B. Check your answer a different way.

   C. Answer: _____

3. Kelli had 9 dolls. She gave some to her sister. Now she has 5 left. How many did she give to her sister?

   A. Model your thinking with a bar diagram.

   B. Check your answer a different way.

   C. Answer: _____

   D. Explain what you did.

4. Joe had 8 marbles. He gave some away and now he has 4. How many did he give away?

   Which equation could you use to solve this problem?

   A. $8 + 4 =$ ____
   B. $8 - 4 =$ ____
   C. None of the above.

5. $10 - 4 =$ ____
   Which story matches this equation?

   A. John had 10 marbles and he got 4 more.
   B. John had 10 marbles and he gave 4 away.
   C. None of the above.

6. The answer is 7 marbles. What is the question?
   Write a subtraction story about 7 marbles.

   A. Problem
   B. Model
   C. Equation

Key Points

- CGI provides a framework for teaching word problems (Carpenter et al., 2014).
- The emphasis should be on the problem types and structure rather than on keywords.
- There are 3 types of *take from* problems.
  - The easiest type of subtraction problem is the *take from result unknown*.
  - A more challenging version is the *take from change unknown*.
  - The most challenging type of subtraction problem is the *take from start unknown*.
- Students should use and be able to describe a variety of models when solving problems.
- Students should use and be able to describe a variety of strategies when solving problems.

Summary

Take from word problems are the second type of problems students learn. They start learning them in Kindergarten and continue learning the problem types from this category through 1st and 2nd grade. Students find the *change unknown* and the *start unknown* problems very challenging. Although the *change unknown* problems are often started in first grade, it is often advised that teachers wait to teach the *start unknown* until the other levels of word problems have been mastered. *Start unknown* problems are the most challenging. All problems should be taught using a variety of models and strategies so that students can explain how they are thinking about the problem and what they are doing with the numbers.

Reflection Questions

1. How do you approach the subtraction problem types?
2. How do you scaffold learning these types with different models and strategies?
3. Do you use technology to teach and practice word problems?
4. What are your biggest takeaways from this chapter?

Reference

Carpenter, T. P., Fennema, E., Franke, M. L., Levi, L., and Empson, S. B. (2014). *Children's mathematics: Cognitively guided instruction* (2nd ed.). Portsmouth, NH: Heinemann.

6

Part-Part-Whole Problems

A *part-part-whole* problem is a problem that discusses the two parts and the whole. There are three types of *part-part-whole* problems (see Figure 6.1). The first is a problem where the *whole* is unknown. For example: *The toy store had 4 big marbles and 5 small marbles. How many marbles do they have altogether?* Another example: *John had $97 in his bank account and $8 in his piggy bank. How much money does he have altogether?* We know both parts and the task is to figure out the whole (see Figures 6.1 through 6.11).

The second kind of problem is a problem where one of the *parts* is unknown. For example: *The toy store had 100 marbles. There were 89 small marbles. The rest of the marbles were large. How many large marbles did they have?* Another example: *Kelly had $50. She had $25 in her piggy bank and the rest in her bank account. How much does she have in her bank account?* In this type of problem, we are given the whole and one of the parts (see Figures 6.12 through 6.20). The task is to figure out the other part.

The third type of problem is a *both addends unknown* problem. In this type of problem both addends are not known; only the total is given (see Figures 6.21 through 6.26). For example: *Jane has 25 cents. Name all the possible coin combinations that she could have.* The task is to figure out all of the possible combinations.

Figure 6.1

Problem Types	Whole Unknown	Part Unknown	Both Addends Unknown
Part-Part-Whole/ Putting Together/ Taking Apart	Marco has 5 red marbles and 5 blue ones. How many marbles does Marco have? 5 + 5 = x	Marco has 10 marbles. Five are red and the rest are blue. How many are blue? 10 − 5 = or 5 + x = 10	Marco has 10 marbles. Some are red and some are blue. How many could be red and how many could be blue?
Bar Diagram Modeling Problem	? [5 | 5]	10 [5 | ?]	10 [? | ?] *Often all of the combinations are represented in a table
What are we looking for? Where is _X_?	In this type of story, we are talking about a group, set or collection of something. Here we know both parts and we are looking for the total.	In this type of story, we are talking about a group, set or collection of something. Here we know the total and one of the parts. We are looking for the amount of the other part.	In this type of story, we are talking about a group, set or collection of something. Here we know the total but we are to think about all the possible ways to make the group, set or collection.
Algebraic Sentence	5 + 5 = ?	5 + ? = 10 10 − 5 = ?	x + y = 10
Strategies to Solve	Add/Count up	Count up/Subtract	Count up/Subtract
Answer	5 + 5 = 10 He had 10 marbles.	5 + 5 = 10 10 − 5 = ? Five were blue.	1 + 9 4 + 6 9 + 1 6 + 4 2 + 8 5 + 5 8 + 2 3 + 7 10 + 0 0 + 10 7 + 3 These are the possibilities.

Part-Part-Whole: Whole Unknown

Concrete Models

Number Frames

Problem: Carlos had 2 small marbles and 2 big marbles. How many does
he have altogether?

Strategy: Doubles

Figure 6.2

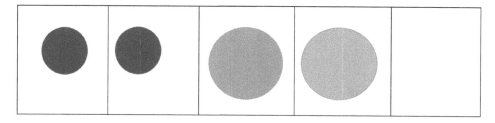

Problem: Anna had 4 small teddy bears and 6 big teddy bears. How
many were there all together?

Strategy: Ten friends

Figure 6.3

Rekenrek

Problem: There were 5 kids upstairs and 5 kids downstairs. How many
                kids were there in the house altogether?
Strategy: Doubles. Use toy cars, stickers or draw cars to model.

Figure 6.4

Pictorial Models

Drawings and Sketches

Problem: Missy had 2 cats and 3 dogs. How many animals does she have
                altogether?
Strategy: Count up

Figure 6.5

Abstract Models

Number Grids

Problem: Jake had 3 big marbles and 7 small marbles. How many does he
have altogether?
Strategy: Ten friends

Figure 6.6

1	2	3	4	5	6	7	8	9	10
11	12	13	14	15	16	17	18	19	20

Problem: Maria had 10 big marbles and 10 small marbles. How many did
she have altogether?
Strategy: Doubles

Figure 6.7

1	2	3	4	5	6	7	8	9	10
11	12	13	14	15	16	17	18	19	20
21	22	23	24	25	26	27	28	29	30
31	32	33	34	35	36	37	38	39	40
41	42	43	44	45	46	47	48	49	50

Problem: Lisa has 25 big marbles and 10 small ones. How many does she
have altogether?
Strategy: Slide 10

Figure 6.8

1	2	3	4	5	6	7	8	9	10
11	12	13	14	15	16	17	18	19	20
21	22	23	24	25	26	27	28	29	30
31	32	33	34	35	36	37	38	39	40
41	42	43	44	45	46	47	48	49	50
51	52	53	54	55	56	57	58	59	60
61	62	63	64	65	66	67	68	69	70
71	72	73	74	75	76	77	78	79	80
81	82	83	84	85	86	87	88	89	90
91	92	93	94	95	96	97	98	99	100

Number Lines

Problem: Lisa had 2 small marbles and 2 big ones. How many did she
              have altogether?
Strategy: Doubles

Figure 6.9

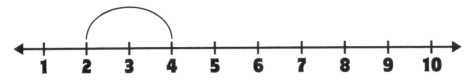

Problem: Tim had 4 small teddy bears and 8 big ones. How many did he
              have altogether?
Strategy: Bridge 10

Figure 6.10

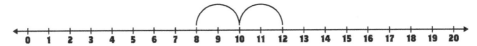

Problem: Greg had 10 small marbles and 40 big marbles. How many did
              he have altogether?
Strategy: Add 10 to a number.

Figure 6.11

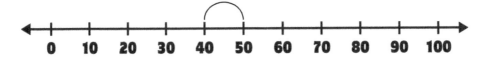

Part-Part-Whole: Part Unknown

Concrete Models

Number Frames

Problem: Carlos had 4 marbles. Carlos had 2 small marbles and some big
marbles. How many big marbles did he have?
Strategy: Doubles

Figure 6.12

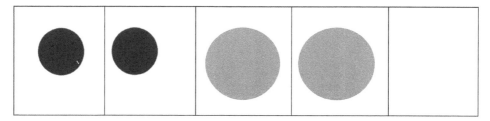

Problem: Anna had 10 teddy bears. Anna had 4 small teddy bears and
some big teddy bears. How many big teddy bears did she have?
Strategy: Ten friends

Figure 6.13

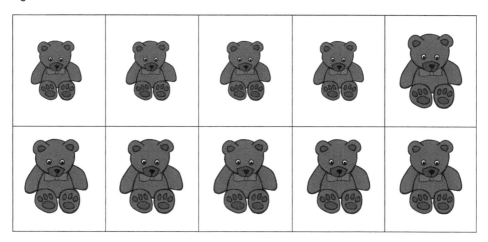

Problem: Jamal had 12 cars. Jamal had 4 small toy cars and some big toy cars. How many big toy cars did he have?

Strategy: Think 4 and what number make 12, or subtract.

Figure 6.14

Pictorial Models

Drawings and Sketches

Problem: Missy had 5 animals. Missy had 2 cats and some dogs. How many dogs did she have?

Strategy: Think 2 and what number make 5.

Figure 6.15

Abstract Models

Number Grids

Problem: Jake had 3 small marbles and some big marbles. He had 10 marbles altogether. How many big ones did he have?
Strategy: Ten friends

Figure 6.16

1	2	3	4	5	6	7	8	9	10
11	12	13	14	15	16	17	18	19	20

Problem: Maria had 20 marbles. She had 10 big marbles and the rest were small marbles. How many small marbles did she have?
Strategy: Doubles

Figure 6.17

1	2	3	4	5	6	7	8	9	10
11	12	13	14	15	16	17	18	19	20
21	22	23	24	25	26	27	28	29	30
31	32	33	34	35	36	37	38	39	40
41	42	43	44	45	46	47	48	49	50

Problem: Lisa had 25 big marbles and some small ones. She had 35 marbles altogether. How many small ones did she have?
Strategy: Slide 10

Figure 6.18

1	2	3	4	5	6	7	8	9	10
11	12	13	14	15	16	17	18	19	20
21	22	23	24	25	26	27	28	29	30
31	32	33	34	35	36	37	38	39	40
41	42	43	44	45	46	47	48	49	50
51	52	53	54	55	56	57	58	59	60
61	62	63	64	65	66	67	68	69	70
71	72	73	74	75	76	77	78	79	80
81	82	83	84	85	86	87	88	89	90
91	92	93	94	95	96	97	98	99	100

Number Lines

Problem: Lisa had 2 small marbles and some big ones. She had 4 marbles
altogether. How many big ones did she have?
Strategy: Doubles

Figure 6.19

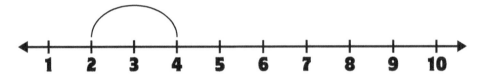

Problem: Tim had 4 small teddy bears and some big ones. He had 12
teddy bears. How many big ones did he have?
Strategy: Bridge 10 (add 6 to get to 10 and then 2 more).

Figure 6.20

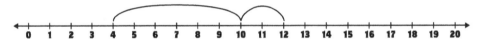

Problem: Greg had 10 small marbles and some big marbles. He had 50
marbles altogether. How many big ones did he have?
Strategy: Subtract 10 from 50

Figure 6.21

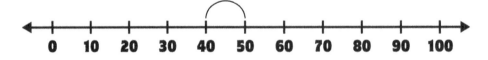

Part-Part-Whole: Both Addends Unknown

Concrete Models

Number Frames (5, 10 and Double 10)

Problem: Marcus had 5 marbles. Some were big and some were small.
　　　　　How many of each could he have had?
Strategy: Act out combinations using number patterns.

Figure 6.22

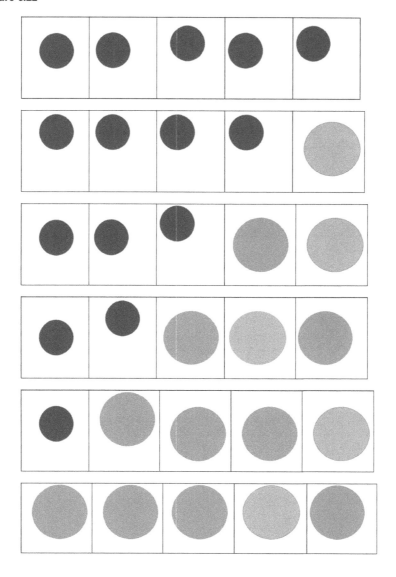

Cubes

Problem: Luke had 7 cars. Some were brown and some were white. How many could he have of each?

Strategy: Act out combinations using number patterns.

Figure 6.23

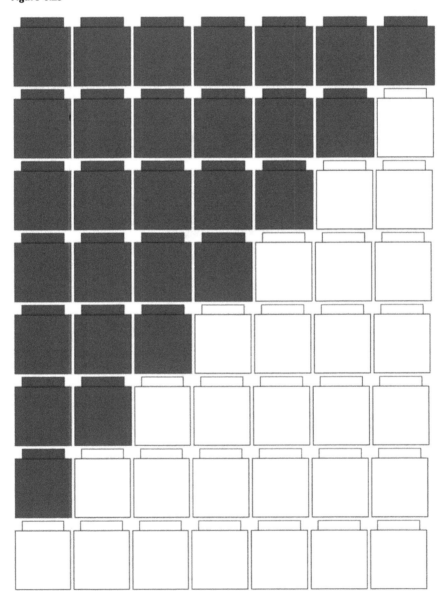

Pictorial Models

Color Templates

Problem: There are 4 birds. Some are pink and some are orange. How many of each color could there be? Color all the possibilities on the template.

Strategy: Color using number patterns.

Figure 6.24

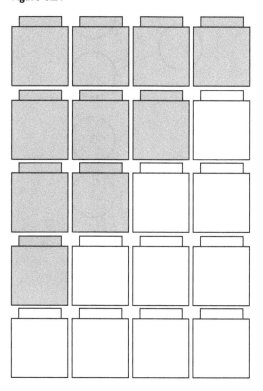

Abstract Models

Number Bond Diagrams

Problem: Marta had 4 rings. Some were pink and some were green. How
many of each color could she have had?
Strategy: Draw number bonds based on number patterns.

Figure 6.25

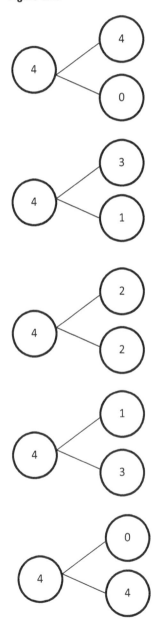

Table

Version 1: Scaffolded

Problem: Raul had 4 animals. Some were cats and some were dogs. How many of each type could he have had?
Strategy: Make a table based on number patterns.

Figure 6.26

Pictures	Cats	Dogs
	4	0
	3	1
	2	2
	1	3
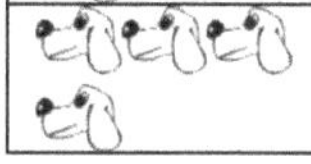	0	4

Version 2: Less Scaffolded

Problem: Raul had 8 candies. Some were sweet and some were sour. How many of each type could he have had?
Strategy: Make a table based on number patterns.

Figure 6.27

Candies	
Sweet	Sour
8	0
7	1
6	2
5	3
4	4
3	5
2	6
1	7
0	8

Assessment

When assessing word problems, it is important to check many aspects (see Figure 6.28). Notice that the following example checks both the easy versions and the harder versions. Check to see if the students can solve one way and check another. Check to see if students can use a variety of models and strategies. Make sure that they can explain what they did. See if they can write the different types of problems as well as solve them.

Figure 6.28

1.	Jamal had 3 green marbles and 4 blue marbles. How many marbles did he have altogether? A. Model your thinking on the 10 frame. B. Model your thinking with a sketch. C. Answer: _____
2.	Mary had 5 rings. Some were big and some were small. How many big and how many small could she have? A. Model your thinking with a picture. B. Model your thinking with a table.
3.	Mark had 5 toy cars. Three were blue and the rest were green. How many were green? A. Model your thinking. B. Check your answer a different way. C. Answer: _____

Key Points

- CGI provides a framework for teaching word problems (Carpenter et al., 2014).
- The emphasis should be on the problem types and structure rather than on keywords.
- There are 3 types of *part-part-whole* problems
    - The easiest type of *part-part-whole* problem is the *whole unknown*.
    - A more challenging version is the *part unknown*.
    - The most challenging type of *part-part-whole* problem is the *both addends unknown*.
- Students should use and be able to describe a variety of models when solving problems.
- Students should use and be able to describe a variety of strategies when solving problems.

Summary

Part-part-whole word problems are learned in kindergarten. They start learning the *whole unknown* versions of these problems. The other two versions are often picked up in 1st grade. However, in the CCSS (2011), kindergarteners are expected to know the *both addends unknown* version of this problem. It is often very difficult but I think that is partly because it isn't connected enough to the composing and decomposing that students are doing throughout the year. If it was, it might be easy for the students to learn these problems. By the end of first grade students should know and be able to explain and solve all the versions of the *part-part-whole* problems. All problems should be taught using a variety of models and strategies so that students can explain how they are thinking about the problem and what they are doing with the numbers.

Reflection Questions

1. How do you approach the *part-part-whole* problem types?
2. How do you scaffold learning these types with different models and strategies?
3. Do you use technology to teach and practice word problems?
4. What are your biggest takeaways from this chapter?

References

Carpenter, T. P., Fennema, E., Franke, M. L., Levi, L., and Empson, S. B. (2014). *Children's mathematics: Cognitively guided instruction* (2nd ed.). Portsmouth, NH: Heinemann.

Common Core Standards Writing Team (2011). *Progressions for the Common Core State Standards in Mathematics (draft).* Retrieved from https://commoncoretools.files.wordpress.com/2011/05/ccss_progression_cc_oa_k5_2011_05_302.pdf.

7

Compare Problems

Comparison Stories

Comparison stories are the most difficult types of stories to tell. There are three types of comparison stories (see Figure 7.1). The first type of comparison story is where two different things are being compared (see Figures 7.2 through 7.8). For example: *Leti had 5 rings and Marta had 7 rings. Who had more? How many more?* Another example: *Mary had $45 and Jane had $35. How much more money does Mary have than Jane?* Or, *How much less money does Jane have than Mary?* In a difference problem, when you say *less*, it is considered a more difficult version of the problem. There is another version of the compare-the-difference problem. For example: *Jean has 20 marbles and Mike has 10. How many more marbles does Mike need to have the same amount as Jean?*

The second type of comparison story is where the bigger part is unknown (see Figures 7.9 through 7.15). In this type of story, we are looking for the bigger amount. For example: *Luke had $57 and Marcos had $19 more than Luke. How much does Marcos have? How much do they have altogether?* Another example: *Luke had $57. This is $10 less than Marcos. How much does Marcos have?* There are two types of this problem. When you say *less* and you are looking for more, it is considered the harder part because it is counterintuitive. The task is to find the bigger part.

The third type of comparison story is where the smaller part is unknown. In this type of story, we are looking for the smaller amount (see Figures 7.16 through 7.22). For example: *Luke had $57 and Marcos had $10 less than Luke. How much does Marcos have? How much do they have altogether?* Another example: *Luke had $57. This is $10 more than Marcos. How much does Marcos have?* There are two types of this problem. When you say *more* and you are looking for the smaller part, it is considered the harder version because it is counterintuitive. The task is to find the smaller part.

Figure 7.1

Problem Types	Difference Unknown	Bigger Part Unknown	Smaller Part Unknown
Compare	Marco has 5 marbles. His brother has 7. How many more marbles does his brother have than he does?	Marco has 5 marbles. His brother has 2 more than he does. How many marbles does his brother have?	Tom has 5 rocks. Marco has 2 fewer than Tom. How many rocks does Marco have?
Bar Diagram Modeling Problem	[5] ? [7]	[5] [5][2] ?	[5] [?][2]
What are we looking for? Where is *X*?	In this type of story, we are comparing two amounts. We are looking for the difference between the two numbers.	In this type of story, we are comparing two amounts. We are looking for the bigger part which is unknown.	In this type of story, we are comparing two amounts. We are looking for the smaller part which is unknown.
Algebraic Sentence	$7 - 5 = ?$	$5 + 2 = ?$	$5 - 2 = ?$
Strategies to Solve	Count up/Count back	Count up	Subtract
Answer	His brother had 2 more marbles than he did.	His brother had 7 marbles.	Marco had 3 marbles.

Compare Difference Unknown

Concrete

Number Frames (5, 10 and Double 10)

Problem: Anna had 4 small teddy bears and 3 big teddy bears. How
many *more* small bears did she have than big ones?
Strategy: Subtract or count up

Figure 7.2

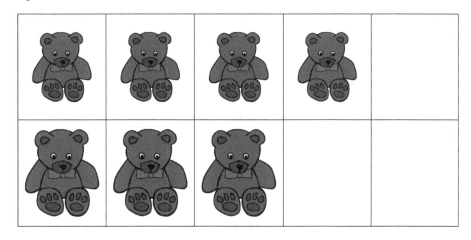

Problem: Lara had 2 marbles. Katie had 4 marbles. How many more marbles does Lara need *to have the same amount* as Katie?
Strategy: Count up

Figure 7.3

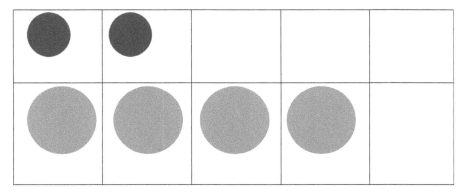

Rekenrek

Problem: Jamal had 10 cars. Tim had 7. How many *fewer* cars did Tim
have than Jamal?
Strategy: Use ten friends, subtract or count up

Figure 7.4

Pictorial

Drawings and Sketches

Problem: Farmer Missy had 15 animals. She had 7 cats and 8 dogs. How
many more dogs did she have than cats?
Strategy: Differences of 1

Figure 7.5

Base 10 Sketch

Problem: Marvin had 41 big marbles and 20 little ones. How many more
big ones did he have than little ones?
Strategy: Compare tens and then ones.

Figure 7.6

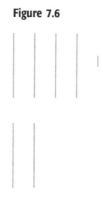

Abstract

Double Number Line

Problem: Tammy had 5 marbles. Celia had 10. Who had more? How
many more?
Strategy: Half facts

Figure 7.7

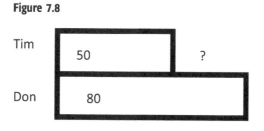

Bar Diagram

Problem: Tim had 50 marbles. Don had 80. How many fewer marbles did
Tim have than Don?
Strategy: Count up tens

Figure 7.8

Tim
50   ?

Don
80

Concrete

Number Frames (5, 10 and Double 10 Frames)

Problem: Anna had 2 small teddy bears and 3 more big teddy bears than small ones. How many big bears did she have?

Strategy: Count on

Figure 7.9

Problem: Lara had 4 marbles. Katie had 1 more marble than she did. How many marbles did Katie have?

Strategy: Count up

Figure 7.10

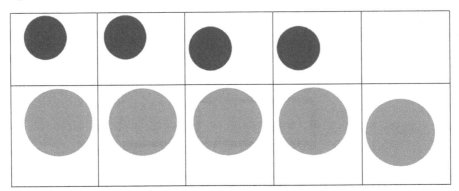

Rekenrek

Problem: Jamal had 5 small toy cars and 5 more big toy cars than small
ones. How many big toy cars did he have?
Strategy: Doubles fact

Figure 7.11

Pictorial

Drawings and Sketches

Problem: Farmer Missy had 4 cats. She had 4 more dogs than cats. How
many dogs did she have?
Strategies: Doubles fact or count up

Figure 7.12

Rekenrek Paper for Drawing Modeling Problem

Figure 7.13

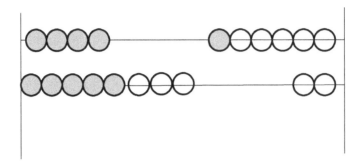

Abstract

Double Number Line

Problem: Tammy had 50 marbles. Celia had 50 more than she did. How many did Celia have?

Strategy: Doubles fact or count up

Figure 7.14

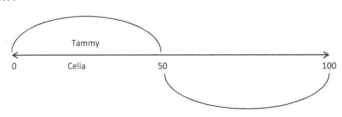

Bar Diagram

Problem: Tim had 50 marbles. He had 30 fewer than Don. How many did Don have?

Strategy: Count up

Figure 7.15

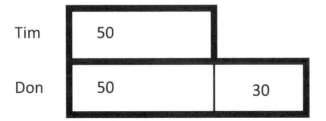

Compare Smaller Part Unknown

Concrete

Number Frames (5, 10 and Double 10)

Problem: Anna had 5 small teddy bears and 3 fewer big teddy bears than
small ones. How many big bears did she have?
Strategy: Subtract

Figure 7.16

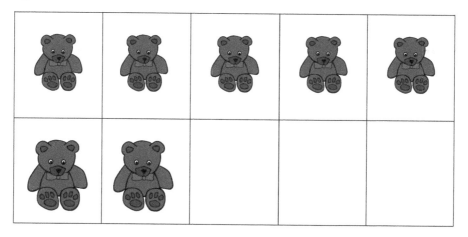

Problem: Lara had 4 marbles. Katie had 1 fewer marble than she did.
How many marbles did Katie have?
Strategy: Subtract

Figure 7.17

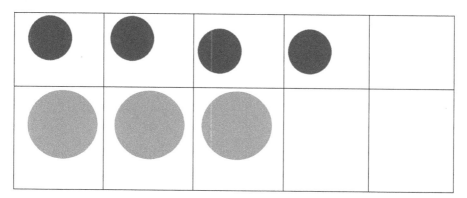

Rekenrek

Problem: Jamal had 7 small toy cars. He had 2 more small toy cars than big ones. How many big toy cars did he have?

Strategy: Subtract

Figure 7.18

Pictorial

Drawings and Sketches

Problem: Farmer Missy had 7 cats. She had 2 fewer dogs than cats. How many dogs did she have?

Strategy: Subtract

Figure 7.19

Rekenrek Paper for Drawing Modeling Problem

Problem: Mary had 5 rings. She had 2 more rings than Kelli. How many rings did Kelli have?

Strategy: Subtract

Figure 7.20

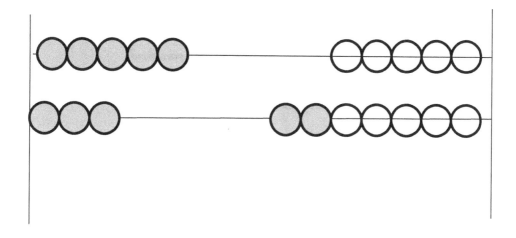

Abstract

Double Number Line

Problem: Tammy had 100 marbles. Celia had 50 fewer marbles than she did. How many did Celia have?

Strategy: Subtract

Figure 7.21

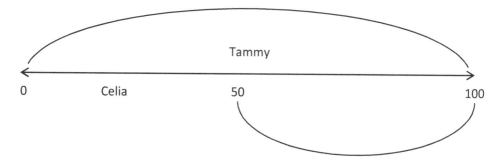

Bar Diagram

Problem: Tim had 80 marbles. He had 40 more than Don. How many did
          Don have?
Strategy: Subtract; also use half facts.

Figure 7.22

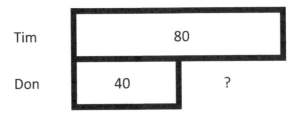

Assessment

When assessing word problems, it is important to check many aspects (Figure 7.23). Notice that the following example checks both the easy versions and the harder versions. Check to see if the students can solve one way and check their work by another. Check to see if students can use a variety of models and strategies. Make sure that they can explain what they did. See if they can write the different types of problems as well as solve them.

Figure 7.23

1. Mary had 10 rings. Sue had 3. How many more rings did Mary have than Sue?

   A. Model your thinking with a sketch.

   B. Model your thinking with a double 10 frame.

   C. Answer: _____

2. Mark had 5 toy cars. Tim had 2 more than he did. How many did Tim have?

   A. Model your thinking.

   B. Check your answer a different way.

   C. Answer: _____

3. Matt had 5 marbles. Ted had 10. How many more marbles does Matt need to have the same amount as Ted?

   A. Model your thinking.

   B. Check your answer a different way.

   C. Answer: _____

4. Kelli had 8 dolls. She had 2 fewer than Kate. How many did Kate have?

   A. Model your thinking.

   B. Check your answer a different way.

   C. Answer: _____

   D. Explain what you did.

5. Raul had 20 candies. Dan had 8 fewer than he did. How many did Dan have?

   A. Model your thinking.

   B. Check a different way.

   C. Answer: _____

   D. Explain what you did.

6. Which equation matches this story?

Lucy has 10 marbles. Jane has 2 fewer than she does. How many does Jane have?

   A. 10 + 2

   B. 10 – 2

   C. None of the above

Key Points

- CGI provides a framework for teaching word problems (Carpenter et al., 2014).
- The emphasis should be on the problem types and structure rather than on keywords.
- There are 3 types of *compare* problems.
- The easiest type of *compare* problem is the *difference unknown*.
  - The *difference unknown* problem has a more difficult version. When using the words *less* or *fewer,* this is considered harder.
- A more challenging version of compare problems is the *bigger part unknown*.
- The most difficult version is *smaller part unknown*.
- The *bigger part unknown* and the *smaller part unknown* questions both have difficult versions. When you say *less* and you are looking for *more*, then this is considered difficult. And, when you say *more* and you are looking for *less*, this is also considered difficult. In the CCSS (2010), these are taught in 2nd grade, or 1st grade if all the other types are learned. In the TEKS (2012), these are all taught in 1st grade. In most other state standards the easy version is taught in 1st and the more difficult version taught in 2nd.
- Students should use and be able to describe a variety of models when solving problems.
- Students should use and be able to describe a variety of strategies when solving problems.

Summary

Compare word problems are taught in 1st grade. Students learn all the versions, but in some states they learn the more challenging versions of these types in the 2nd grade. By the end of 1st grade, students should know and be able to explain and solve all the easy versions of the *compare* problems. All problems should be taught using a variety of models and strategies so that students can explain how they are thinking about the problem and what they are doing with the numbers.

Reflection Questions

1. How do you approach the *compare* problem types?
2. How do you scaffold learning these types with different models and strategies?

3. Do you use technology to teach and practice word problems?
4. What are your biggest takeaways from this chapter?

References

Carpenter, T. P., Fennema, E., Franke, M. L., Levi, L., and Empson, S. B. (2014). *Children's mathematics: Cognitively guided instruction* (2nd ed.). Portsmouth, NH: Heinemann.

Math Learning Center.org. (2017). "Number Rack for iPad, Web, and More." Available at http://www.mathlearningcenter.org/web-apps/number-rack/

National Governors Association Center for Best Practices and Council of Chief State School Officers (CCSS). (2010). *Common core state standards for mathematics.* Washington, DC: Authors.

Texas Essential Knowledge of Mathematics (TEKS). (2012). Retrieved on November 1, 2016 from http://ritter.tea.state.tx.us/rules/tac/chapter111/

8

Two-Step Problems and More

After students have mastered solving one-step problems, they start working on two-step problems and then multi-step problems (see Figures 8.1 through 8.21). The hierarchy of these problems is often not attended to in teaching. This is highly detrimental to student learning because two-step and multi-step problems are simply one-step problems with two or more parts. It is important to remember to scaffold levels of difficulty so that the cognitive load is balanced. Don't give hard problems with hard numbers to start with because then students become cognitively overloaded.

Give hard problem types with easy numbers so that students can focus on the problem. Once they know how to solve the problem, then give harder numbers. Often the problem is that students don't fully understand one of the parts, so it is crucial that students understand the one-step problems before they go on to others. This must be assessed and addressed on an ongoing basis. Many researchers (Powell, 2011) discuss multi-step word problems, however the CCSS does a great job of describing the trajectory in the Counting and Cardinality Math Progressions (Common Core Standards Writing Team, 2011, p. 18).

Figure 8.1

Level 1	Level 2	Level 3	Level 4	Level 5
Same Operation	Different Operations	Combined Compare	Mixed Levels	Mixed Levels of Harder Versions
Sue had $5. For her birthday, her mother gives her $14 and her brother gives her $10. How much money does she have now?	Sue had $5. She gives her sister $2. Her dad gives her $4 more. How much money does she have now?	Sue had $3. Her sister had $1 less than she did. How much money did they have altogether?	On the farm there were 10 animals. There were 5 sheep and some horses. Then, the farmer bought 5 more horses. How many horses are there now? How many animals are there altogether now?	On the farm there were 10 animals. There were 5 sheep and some horses. The farmer bought more horses. Now there are 10 horses. How many horses did the farmer buy? How many animals are there altogether now?

Level 1: Same Operation

Concrete Models

Number Frames

Problem: Jamal had 4 marbles. He got 2 more from his brother and 10
more from his parents. How many does he have now?
Strategy: Doubles fact

Figure 8.2

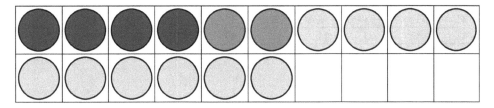

Pictorial Models

Drawings and Sketches

Problem: Missy had 4 dolls. She got 3 more. Then she got 5 more. How
many does she have now?
Strategy: Add

Figure 8.3

Abstract Models

Number Grids

Problem: Maria had 22 marbles. She got 15 more. Then she got 10 more. How many does she have now?

Strategy: Use number grid slides. Slide down 10 and over 5 and then down 10. Also you could add tens and then add ones.

Figure 8.4

1	2	3	4	5	6	7	8	9	10
11	12	13	14	15	16	17	18	19	20
21	22	23	24	25	26	27	28	29	30
31	32	33	34	35	36	37	38	39	40
41	42	43	44	45	46	47	48	49	50

Number Lines

Problem: Greg had 50 marbles. He got 20 more and then 30 more. How many does he have now?

Strategy: Jumping tens

Figure 8.5

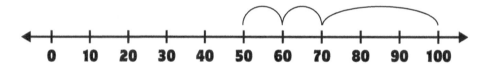

Problem: Marline had 34 marbles. She got 27 more and then 10 more. How many does she have now?

Strategy: Count up to a friendly number and then on from there.

Figure 8.6

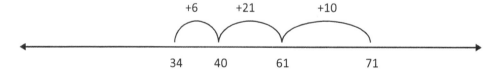

Level 2: Different Operations

Concrete Models

Number Frames

Problem: Jamal had 4 marbles. He gave 2 away. Then his brother gave him 10 more. How many does he have now?

Strategy: Subtracting and then adding 10 to a number

Figure 8.7

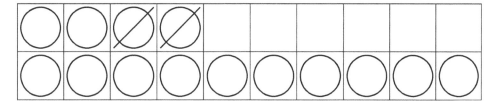

Pictorial Models

Drawings and Sketches

Problem: Missy had 4 dolls. She gave 2 to her sister. Then she got 5 more. How many does she have now?

Strategy: Add

Figure 8.8

Abstract Models

Number Grids

Problem: Maria had 22 marbles. She gave 10 away. Then she got 7 more.
How many does she have now?
Strategy: Use number grid slides. Slide up 10 and then over 7.

Figure 8.9

1	2	3	4	5	6	7	8	9	10
11	12	13	14	15	16	17	18	19	20
21	22	23	24	25	26	27	28	29	30
31	32	33	34	35	36	37	38	39	40
41	42	43	44	45	46	47	48	49	50

Number Lines

Problem: Greg had 50 marbles. He gave away 20. Then he got 30 more.
How many does he have now?
Strategy: Jumping tens

Figure 8.10

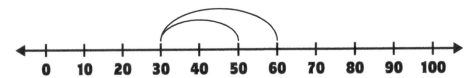

Problem: Marta had 34 marbles. She gave 17 away. Then she got 10 more
and then 10 more. How many does she have now?
Strategy: Count up to a friendly number and then on from there.

Figure 8.11

Level 3: Combined Compare

Concrete Models

Number Frames

Problem: Jamal had 4 marbles. His sister had 2 more than he did. How many do they have altogether?
Strategy: Count up

Figure 8.12

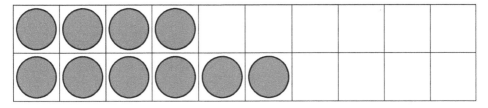

Pictorial Models

Drawings and Sketches

Problem: Missy had 4 dolls. Her sister had 2 fewer than she did. How many did they have altogether?
Strategy: Add

Figure 8.13

Abstract Models

Number Grids

Problem: Maria had 22 marbles. Her friend Lucy had 10 more than she
did. How many did they have altogether?

Strategy: Use number grid slides. Start at 22 and slide down 22 and then
10 more.

Figure 8.14

1	2	3	4	5	6	7	8	9	10
11	12	13	14	15	16	17	18	19	20
21	22	23	24	25	26	27	28	29	30
31	32	33	34	35	36	37	38	39	40
41	42	43	44	45	46	47	48	49	50
51	52	53	54	55	56	57	58	59	60

Tape Diagram

Figure 8.15

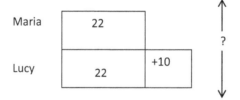

Level 4: Mixed Levels

Concrete Models

Number Frames

Problem: There were 10 animals. 5 were cows and the rest were horses.
Then 2 more horses came.
(Two-step) How many horses are there now?
(Multi-step) How many animals are there altogether?
Strategy: Count up

Figure 8.16

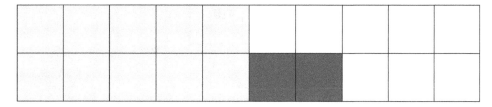

Pictorial Models

Drawings and Sketches

Problem: Farmer Joe had 3 cats and some dogs. He had 6 animals. Then
he got 5 more dogs.
(Two-step) How many dogs does he have now?
(Multi-step) How many animals does he have altogether?
Strategy: Add

Figure 8.17

Abstract Models

Tape Diagram

Problem: Farmer Joe had 30 cats and some dogs. He had 60 animals.
Then he got 10 more dogs.
(Two-step) How many dogs does he have now?
(Multi-step) How many animals does he have altogether?
Strategy: Add

Figure 8.18

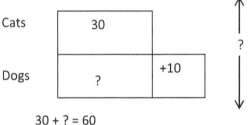

30 + ? = 60

30 + 10 = 40 He has 40 dogs.

30 + 40 = 70 He has 70 animals altogether.

Concrete Models

Number Frames

Problem: There were 10 animals. 5 were cows and the rest were horses. Then some more horses came. Now there are 10 horses. (Two-step) How many horses came? (Multi-step) How many animals are there altogether?

Strategy: Count up

Figure 8.19

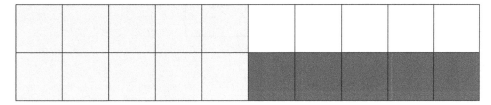

Pictorial Models

Drawings and Sketches

Problem: Farmer Joe had 3 cats and some dogs. He had 6 animals. Then he got some more dogs. Now he has 10 dogs. (Two-step) How many dogs did he get? (Multi-step) How many animals does he have altogether?

Strategy: Add

Figure 8.20

Abstract Models

Tape Diagram

Problem: Farmer Joe had 20 cats and some dogs. He had 40 animals.
Then he got some more dogs. Now he has 50 dogs. How many
dogs did he get? How many animals does he have altogether?

Strategy: Add

Figure 8.21

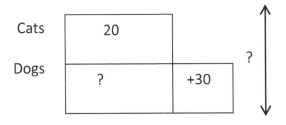

20 + ? = 40

20 + 30 = 50 He got 30 dogs.

20 + 50 = 70 He has 70 animals altogether.

Assessment

When assessing word problems, it is important to check many aspects.
Notice that the following example checks both the easy versions and the
harder versions. Check to see if the students can solve one way and check
another. Check to see if students can use a variety of models and strategies. Make sure that they can explain what they did. See if they can write
the different types of problems as well as solve them.

Figure 8.22

1. Mary had 5 rings. She got 7 more and then 3 more. How many does she have now?

    A. Model your thinking with a sketch.

    B. Model your thinking with a double 10 frame.

    C. Answer: _____

2. Mark had 5 toy cars. He gave Tim 3. His cousin gave him 10. How many does he have now?

    A. Model your thinking.

    B. Check your answer a different way.

    C. Answer: _____

3. Kelli had 10 dolls. She had 2 fewer than Kate. How many did they have altogether?

    A. Model your thinking.

    B. Check your answer a different way.

    C. Answer:_____

    D. Explain what you did.

4. There were 50 kids on the playground. Twenty-five were boys and the rest were girls. Then 10 more girls came. How many girls are there now? How many students are there altogether now?

    A. Model your thinking.

    B. Model your thinking another way.

    C. Explain how you know that your answer is correct.

1	2	3	4	5	6	7	8	9	10
11	12	13	14	15	16	17	18	19	20
21	22	23	24	25	26	27	28	29	30
31	23	33	34	35	36	37	38	39	40
41	42	43	44	45	46	47	48	49	50
51	52	53	54	55	56	57	58	59	60
61	62	63	64	65	66	67	68	69	70

25 + ? = 50
25 +10 = 35 There are 35 girls now.
50 + 10 = 60 There are 60 students altogether.

5. There were 40 kids on the playground. Twenty-five were girls and the rest were boys. Some more boys came. Now there are 30 boys. How many boys came?

   A. Model your thinking with a tape diagram.

   B. Check a different way.

   C. Answer: _____

   D. Explain what you did.

Key Points

- The emphasis should be on the problem types and structure rather than on keywords.
- There are 5 types of two-step problems.
- There is a hierarchy of two-step problems.
  - The first level is *same operation*.
  - The second level is *different operations*.
  - The third level is *compare*.
  - The fourth and fifth levels are *mixed problem types*.
- Multi-step problems can be extensions of two-step problems.
- Students should use and be able to describe a variety of models when solving problems.
- Students should use and be able to describe a variety of strategies when solving problems.

Summary

There are a variety of two-step problems. Students start to explore these problems during 2nd grade. It is important that teachers consider the hierarchy and scaffold from the easiest levels to the more difficult levels. It is important to remember when introducing problems to give easy numbers so that students can focus on solving the problem. After students learn how to solve the problem, then they can work with more difficult numbers.

Reflection Questions

1. How do you approach the two-step problem types?
2. How do you scaffold learning these types with different models and strategies?
3. Do you use technology to teach and practice word problems?
4. What are your biggest takeaways from this chapter?

References

Common Core Standards Writing Team (2011). Progressions for the Common Core State Standards in Mathematics (draft). Retrieved on December 16, 2016 from https://commoncoretools.files. wordpress.com/2011/05/ccss_progression_cc_oa_k5_2011_05_302. pdf

Powell, S. (2011). Solving word problems using schemas: a review of the literature. *Learning Disabilities Research & Practice*, *26*(2), 94–108. Retrieved on December 16, 2016 from https://www.ncbi.nlm.nih. gov/pmc/articles/PMC3105905/

9

Problem Solving Across Math Topics

There are many different types of word problems that students should be able to solve. They should be able to use frameworks to solve odd and even problems, array problems, money and time problems (see Figures 9.1 through 9.12).

Operations and Algebraic Thinking

Odd and Even Problems

1. Jan is having a dinner. She will invite 7 people. Will she need an odd number of chairs or an even number of chairs?
    A. Explain your thinking with concrete models in the 10 frame.

    Figure 9.1

    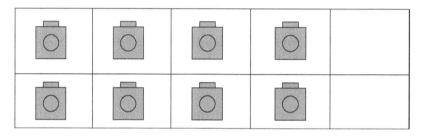

    B. Explain your thinking with drawings.

    Figure 9.2

2. Five girls are standing in a line. The teacher told them to get in pairs. Does every girl have a partner? Is 5 an odd or an even number?
    A. Explain your thinking with concrete models in the 10 frame.

    Figure 9.3

    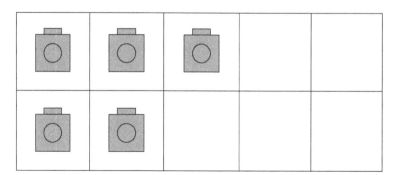

B. Explain your thinking with drawings.

Figure 9.4

Array Problems

1. The bakery had 5 rows of cupcakes. They had 3 cupcakes in each row. How many cupcakes did they have altogether?
   A. Explain your thinking with concrete models.

Figure 9.5

X	X	X		
X	X	X		
X	X	X		
X	X	X		
X	X	X		

B. Explain your thinking with a sketch.

Figure 9.6

C. Explain your thinking with a tape diagram.

Figure 9.7

Cupcakes in a row

3
3
3
3
3

?

D. Write an equation to show your thinking.
   $3 + 3 + 3 + 3 + 3 = 15$

10 More and 10 Less and 100 More and 100 Less; Adding or Subtracting Multiples of 10

Explain your thinking with base 10 blocks.

Problem: Juan had $70. He spent $20. How much does he have left?
Strategy: Count back 20.

Figure 9.8

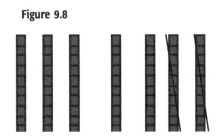

Play Money

Explain your thinking with play money.

Figure 9.9

Number Grids

Explain your thinking with pictures or sketches.

Problem: Marta had 30 marbles. She got 10 more. How many does she have now?

Strategy: Count up 10. Shade in the number grid to show adding 30 + 10.

Figure 9.10

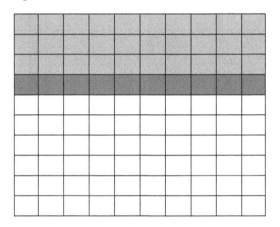

More Number Grids

Problem: Lucy had $145. She spent $100. How much does she have left?
Strategy: Find the difference between 45 and 145. Count up or back.

Figure 9.11

1	2	3	4	5	6	7	8	9	10
11	12	13	14	15	16	17	18	19	20
21	22	23	24	25	26	27	28	29	30
31	32	33	34	35	36	37	38	39	40
41	42	43	44	45	46	47	48	49	50
51	52	53	54	55	56	57	58	59	60
61	62	63	64	65	66	67	68	69	70
71	72	73	74	75	76	77	78	79	80
81	82	83	84	85	86	87	88	89	90
91	92	93	94	95	96	97	98	99	100
101	102	103	104	105	106	107	108	109	110
111	112	113	114	115	116	117	118	119	120
121	122	123	124	125	126	127	128	129	130
131	132	133	134	135	136	137	138	139	140
141	142	143	144	145	146	147	148	149	150
151	152	153	154	155	156	157	158	159	160
161	162	163	164	165	166	167	168	169	170
171	172	173	174	175	176	177	178	179	180
181	182	183	184	185	186	187	188	189	190
191	192	193	194	195	196	197	198	199	200

Bar Diagram

Problem: Marta had 250 marbles. She gave away 100. How many marbles does she have now?
Strategy: Subtract or add up.

Figure 9.12

Start

250	
100	?

Gave away   Left

Money Problems

Money problems are difficult for students. Money is a part of students' everyday lives. Make sure that you use play money to teach these stories. Students need to actually hold and count and reason about money using the play money. They need to do 2 and 3 step problems involving all of the operations by actually acting them out. First, we need to teach students to identify what type of problem they are working with (see Figures 9.13 through 9.18). Next we need to teach them how to model the problem in different ways.

Figure 9.13

<table>
<tr><td colspan="8" align="center">Money Word Problem Types</td></tr>
<tr>
<th>Result Unknown</th>
<th>Change Unknown</th>
<th>Start Unknown</th>
<th>Part-Part-Whole: Whole Unknown</th>
<th>Part-Part-Whole: Part Unknown</th>
<th>Compare Difference Unknown</th>
<th>Compare Bigger Part Unknown</th>
<th>Compare Smaller Part Unknown</th>
</tr>
<tr>
<td>Joel had $58. He got $34 more for his birthday. How much does he have now?</td>
<td>Tom had $40. He saved some more. Now he has $100. How much did he save?</td>
<td>Mike had some money. He got $23 more. Now he has $70. How much did he have in the beginning?</td>
<td>Maribel had 3 quarters and 2 dimes. How much money did she have altogether?</td>
<td>Joel went to the store with $90. He spent $65 on clothes. He spent the rest on shoes. How much did he spend on shoes?</td>
<td>Sue had $57. Luke had $20. How much more money did Sue have than Luke?

Or

How much less money did Luke have than Sue? How much do they have altogether?</td>
<td>Kay has $45. Lucy has $20 more than her. How much money does Lucy have? How much do they have altogether?

Or

Kay has $45. She has $20 less than Lucy. How much does Lucy have? How much do they have altogether?</td>
<td>Sue had $78. She had $12 more than Luke. How much did Luke have? How much do they have altogether?

Or

Sue had $78. Luke had $9 less than she did. How much did he have? How much do they have altogether?</td>
</tr>
</table>

Students are expected to be able to solve word problems about money with $ and ¢. They can do this with either a number line or drawings of the money. *For example: Sue had 1 quarter and 2 dimes. How much money did she have altogether?*

Figure 9.14

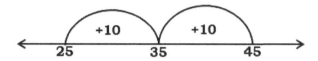

A soda, hamburger and French fries cost $6. The soda cost $1 more than the French fries. The hamburger was $1 more than the soda. What was the cost of each thing?

Model with a bar diagram:

Figure 9.15

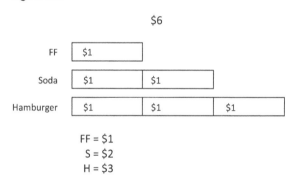

The bakery is selling delicious treats. They are selling pies for $5 apiece, cookies for $3 apiece and cupcakes for $2 apiece.

Figures 9.16, 9.17 and 9.18

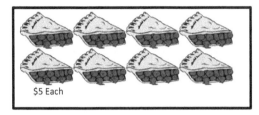

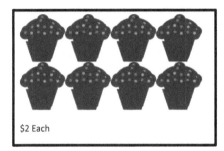

1. What is the most expensive treat?
2. What is the least expensive treat?
3. Which costs more, 3 pieces of pie or 4 cookies?
4. If Kate bought 1 of each treat, how much would she spend?
5. Luke bought 2 pieces of pie and Kate bought 4 cookies. Who spent more money? How much more money?
6. Tim bought 14 cupcakes. Matt bought 2 fewer cupcakes than Tim. Kate bought 4 more cupcakes than Tim. Make a bar diagram to show this story. How many cupcakes did each person buy? How many did they buy altogether? How much money did they spend?

Drawing with a Ruler

Many state standards now actually state that 2nd graders should know how to illustrate their mathematical thinking about measurement through drawings (including rulers). This is very interesting, given that this is not a part of many textbook curriculums. Therefore, it is important to include these types of problems in a unit of study. For example: *Stacy is creating her own deck of cards. She wants to make jumbo cards. She is going to make cards that are 7 inches by 7 inches. Can you draw her card?*

Data Problems

In most standards 2nd grade students are expected to start working with line plots (see Figures 9.19 through 9.24).

Line Plots

The 2nd grade made a frequency table of pets per person in their class. Use the data in the frequency table to make a line plot.

Figure 9.19

Pets Per Person	
Zero Pets	7
1 Pet	5
2 Pets	6
3 Pets	4
4 Pets	2

Figure 9.20

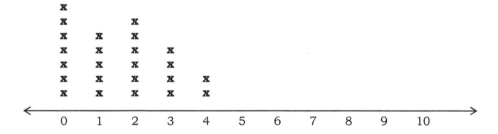

Line plot of pets per person in our classroom

Line Plot Questions:

1. How many people voted altogether?
2. How many more people have no pets than have 2 pets?
3. How many fewer people have 4 pets than have 1 pet?

Bar Graphs

Second grade students are expected to use data to make a bar graph and then be able to answer questions framed around the different problem types. See the following example (Figures 9.21, 9.22, 9.23, 9.24):

The 2nd grade voted on their favorite animals. Use the data in the frequency table to make a bar graph.

Figure 9.21

Favorite Animals	
Birds	20
Cats	40
Dogs	50
Reptiles	30
Other	25

Figure 9.22

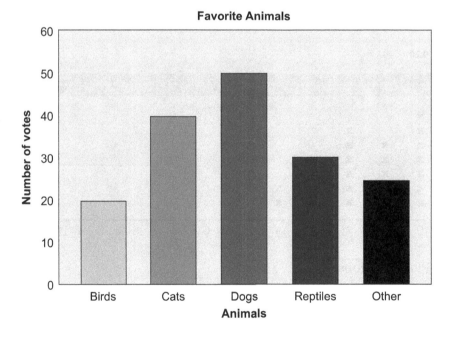

Bar Graph Questions:

1. How many people voted altogether?
2. How many more people liked cats than birds?
3. How many fewer people liked birds than dogs?

Picture Graphs

Second grade students are expected to use data to make a picture graph and then be able to answer questions about it.

See the following example:

The 2nd grade voted on their favorite animals. Use the data in the frequency table to make a picture graph.

Figure 9.23

Favorite Animals	
Birds	20
Cats	40
Dogs	50
Reptiles	30
Other	25

Figure 9.24

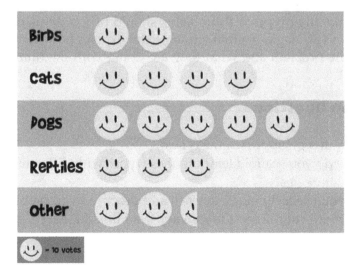

Favorite Animals

Picture Graph

Picture Graph Questions:

1. How many people voted altogether?
2. How many more people liked cats than birds?
3. How many fewer people liked reptiles than liked dogs?

Key Points

- There are different types of problems across math topics.
- There are even and odd problems.
- There are array problems.
- There are place value problems.
- There are money problems.
- There are measurement problems.
- Students should use and be able to describe a variety of models when solving problems.
- Students should use and be able to describe a variety of strategies when solving problems.

Summary

It is important to incorporate various word problems as they come up during the year. It is important to frame them around the CGI framework. This means that teachers are making explicit connections between the problem types as they are solving them with measurement problems, data problems and other types. All problems should be taught using a variety of models and strategies so that students can explain how they are thinking about the problem and what they are doing with the numbers.

Reflection Questions

1. How do you approach the types?
2. How do you scaffold learning these types with different models and strategies?
3. Do you use technology to teach and practice word problems?
4. What are your biggest takeaways from this chapter?

Part III
Other Word Problems

10

Reasoning about Problems

Students can engage in really sophisticated problem posing when given situations that they are interested in and understand.

Building reasoning skills in young children is an essential element of teaching math in the primary grades. Reasoning is one of the 5 elements of being a mathematically proficient student. Students must learn to "think logically about the relationships among concepts and situations" (Kilpatrick, Swafford and Findell, 2001, p. 129). Students need to be able to think about different ways to approach the problem, if their answer makes sense, and how they can verify and justify their answers. It all starts in the primary grades. Students must learn to explain their thinking and prove their thinking in many ways. They should be encouraged to look at and think about patterns and relationships among numbers (Kilpatrick et al., 2001). Students should be encouraged to use both "mental and physical representations" as "tools to think with" (Kilpatrick et al., 2001).

Tools matter. They scaffold thinking and help students to reason about the math they are doing. It allows students to stretch their own thinking. Kilpatrick, Swafford and Findell note that "with the help of representation-building experiences, children can demonstrate sophisticated reasoning abilities" (2001, p. 130). Students should be given time to work alone, in pairs and in small groups to act out the math, show it with manipulatives, and make sketches and drawings. They should be comfortable with showing their thinking using diagrams, tables and other models. We have to model for them how to do these things and explain their thinking as well as listen to the thinking of others. We must constantly be scaffolding the language that they are using to talk about math in meaningful ways.

Contextualizing

Students should not only solve problems but also pose them. It actually is not that difficult to get students to pose problems, but you have to scaffold them. For example, last December I was in a kindergarten classroom, working on posing problems. I started by telling problems about marbles. The kids just didn't really get it and were not actively responding. The teacher whispered in my ear that they had been talking about Santa Claus and elves. So, I began to tell subtraction stories about how Mrs. Claus made some cookies and then how Santa and the elves ate them. What a difference a topic makes. The students took off immediately.

Everyone was able to tell a story, they were really excited and the stories became very sophisticated. See, students will take leaps if they understand what they are doing and feel comfortable. Here is a sample student story: *Mrs. Santa made 7 cookies. Santa ate 2, the girl elf ate 1 and the boy elf ate 1. How many cookies did they eat altogether? How many were left?*

To get students to make up word problems, they need a context. Give them a context and they will give you a story. This takes time and practice and storytelling mats. Storytelling mats are just mats that have a context, like flowers, a barn, an ocean. I use both pre-made ones as well as ones that the students make. The research shows that when students make their own mats, they really enjoy them and personalize them.

Another way to get students to tell stories is to give students the context at first. For example, tell the students that the answer is 5 cookies and ask them "What is the question?" Sometimes, I tell the students what type of problem it is. This is different from just saying the answer is 5. At first, you might tell the students it's an addition problem or a subtraction problem and have them practice those.

Using Templates to Scaffold Problem Solving

Templates help to scaffold the process as well. Templates are laid out step-by-step so that students don't miss any of the process. The templates hold the students responsible for all the parts of writing word problems. Notice that in the templates there is an emphasis on a set-up equation and a solution equation. Part of the reasoning is that students understand how to show the problem with equations.

Equations

Students should know how to write a symbol for the unknown in a problem in first grade. I use symbols (empty box, happy face, empty line) and

Figure 10.1

Template A
Write the problem.
Now make a picture in your head of this problem.

What type of problem is this? Addition Subtraction Part-Part-Whole Compare	What are we looking for? Write an equation with a symbol for the part that we are looking for.
Model the problem with a sketch.	

Write the equation with the missing number in it.
Answer: _____units

I also use letters. I don't use x because that is too abstract for younger students. But I do use a letter that stands for the thing we are talking about. So for example, if the problem is about *marbles*, we would use an *m*. Students understand that. There tends to be an over-emphasis on the solution equation and not enough on the set-up equation. These are equally important. The set-up equation actually helps to set up the problem. It allows students to really identify what they are looking for. If students know what they are looking for, they are much more likely to find it. When students read a problem and visualize it, the next thing they need to do is verbalize it and determine what they are looking for. Then, they can write an equation with a symbol to show that. That is an essential step in teaching problem solving.

Figure 10.2

Template B
Write the problem.
Make a picture in your head of the problem.

What type of problem is this? Is it a 1-step or 2-step?	What are we looking for? Write an equation with a symbol for the part that we are looking for.
Model the problem with a sketch.	

Check the problem another way:
Write the equation(s) with the missing number in it.   Answer: _____units

Using Graphic Organizers to Write a Word Problem

Work with structure—meaning, work on a specific type of word problem (see Figures 10.3 and 10.4). For example, you could tell the students you are going to work on addition problems. Then, on the board, do a group graphic organizer of all the elements of the word problem.

Problem 1: There were 5 students on the playground. Two more students came. How many kids are there now?
Problem 2: The bakery had 10 cupcakes. Then they made some more. Now they have 20 cupcakes. How many did they make?

Figure 10.3

Setting	Things	What do you know?	What are you looking for?
Playground	Swings/Slides	Start	Start
Classroom	Students	Change	Change
Cafeteria	Cupcakes	End	End
Bus	Cookies		
Bakery			

Figure 10.4

Write the problem.	Write the question.
Model your thinking. **Write the set-up equation.**	**Write the equation.**

More Routines for "*What is the Question?*"

The teacher can hang a poster at the beginning of the week and write: *The answer is 12 marbles. Write a word problem for this answer.* Throughout the week the students can write problems and put them on post-its to answer the problem. Teachers can also do this activity in small, guided-math groups or post this as a workstation activity.

Another Version of "*What is the Question?*"

There is a great deal of research around getting students to actually think about the problem situation. In these problems, the student is given the word problem but not the question. The idea is that if students focus on the problem and understand the scenario, then they will intuitively know what the question should be. For example: *The toy store has 50 marbles. They got a shipment of 50 more.* Here is where students are supposed to come up with the question. This is a great way to see if students are reasoning about the problem. Here is another example: *Miguel ate 2 pieces of candy in the afternoon. In the evening he ate another 2 pieces of candy. What could be the question?*

Two- and Three-Bean Salad Problems

There is a famous set of problems out of the Lawrence Hall of Science (2007) in Berkeley California that looks at developing algebraic reasoning through what is called two- or three-bean salad problems (Figures 10.5 through 10.10). Many people have taken this idea and done a great deal of work with it. I like the problems because they are engaging, hands-on and rigorous. Students start out with simple problems that get progressively more difficult. See Figures 10.5 and 10.6 for examples.

The absolutely most fantastic thing about the two- and three-bean salad problems is that they scaffold nicely into a bar diagram. So, the students solve with the beans. Then they draw a picture of what they solved. Then they put a rectangle around that picture. Then they take out the beans and just put numbers and label the rectangles. Voila! A bar diagram. Of course, you don't teach all of this at once. But you scaffold into the bar diagram.

Figure 10.5

2-bean problem:
There are 2 types of beans.

There are 5 red beans and some black beans. There are 10 beans in all. How many black beans are there?

1. Act out the problems.
2. Draw the beans.
3. Make a bar diagram.

Figure 10.6

3-bean problem: There are 10 beans. Half of them are red beans. Two of them are brown and the rest are black beans. How many of each are there?

1. Use the beans to solve.

2. Draw a sketch of the beans.

3. Make a bar diagram.

Figure 10.7

Mike had some beans. Three were white beans. He had 1 fewer red bean than white beans. He had 2 more black beans than red beans. How many of each bean was there? How many beans were there altogether?

Step 1: Act out the bean problem.
Step 2: Draw out the beans.
Step 3: Put the beans in a rectangle.

Figure 10.8

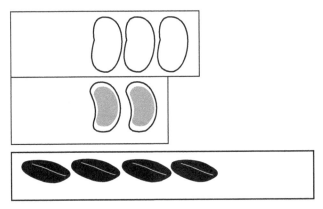

Step 4: Draw the rectangle with just the numbers and labels.

Figure 10.9

White beans	3
Red beans	2
Black beans	4

Coin Puzzle Problems

There are also coin puzzle problems (Lawrence Hall of Science, 2007) that elicit the same type of reasoning but using coins as a pretext rather than beans. Students should be encouraged to use physical models as well as drawings, diagrams and tables to work through the possibilities.

Figure 10.10

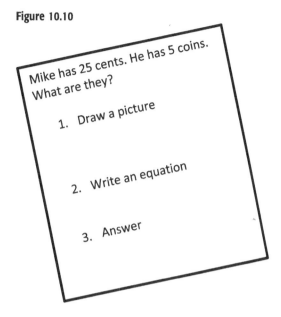

Word Problem Sort

In this workstation, the students sort the word problem by category (see Figure 10.11). This station helps students to reason about the type of problem they are solving. It is very important that students understand and can explain the situation. Although they might use an inverse operation or another strategy to solve the problem, they need to understand the problem situation. For example, I might use subtraction to solve an addition problem but that doesn't change the problem type. The strategy to solve the problem might have been subtraction, but the problem is still an addition type.

Figure 10.11

Word Problem Sort	
Addition	Subtraction
Marta had 4 red rings and she got 2 blue ones. How many does she have now?	Marta had 4 red rings. She gave 2 to her sister. How many does she have now?

Concentration Match

There are different versions of concentration match (see Figures 10.12 and 10.13). One version is where the students match the expression to the correct problem. The other version is the students find the story that goes with an expression. Students need to be able to write the expression and/or equation that matches a problem because it shows that they can reason about the numbers—going from words to numbers. They also need to be able to reason from the numbers and be able to think about which situations match this problem (thus going from numbers to words).

Figure 10.12

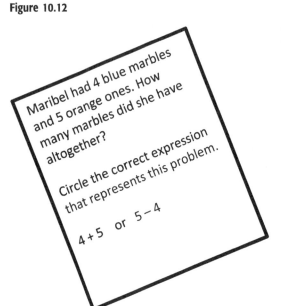

Maribel had 4 blue marbles and 5 orange ones. How many marbles did she have altogether?

Circle the correct expression that represents this problem.

4 + 5   or   5 – 4

Figure 10.13

15 – 3

Circle a story that could match this expression.

a. There were 15 kids in the class. 3 left.
b. There are 18 kids in the class and 3 left.
c. There were 15 kids in the house and 3 more came.
d. None of the above.

Matrix Problems

Matrix problems scaffold logical thinking for students (see Figure 10.14). They have a place to track what they are doing and think about and record all the information they are getting. We need to bring back these types of problems into our classrooms because they promote logical, step-by-step thinking with a lot of different information. It is a skill to be able to think this way and these types of matrices build that skill.

Kelly and her 2 friends stopped by the bakery after studying in the library. They each bought a cookie. Their names are Kelly, Sue and Jamal. The types of cookies were oatmeal, chocolate and strawberry.

Use these clues to tell who ate which cookie.

Kelly only likes fruit.
Sue loves chocolate.
Jamal loves all types of cookies.

Figure 10.14

	Strawberry	Oatmeal	Chocolate
Kelly	x		
Sue			x
Jamal		x	

Venn Diagrams are Great Thinking Activities

Venn diagrams also provide a way for students to think about a lot of different information (see Figures 10.15 and 10.16). We need to also bring these back into our routines so that students learn to organize information and then think about it in clear ways. Students should start out with easy Venn diagrams, using concrete materials to act out the problems, and then move on to representational ones with pictures and then just numbers.

Example 1:

There are 20 students. 7 students like pumpkin pie and 8 like apple pie. 5 students like both.

1. **How many students like only pumpkin pie?**
2. **How many students like only apple pie?**
3. **How many students don't like either one?**

Figure 10.15

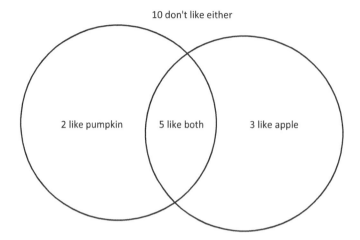

10 don't like either

2 like pumpkin   5 like both   3 like apple

Explain your thinking: *There are 20 students. If 7 like pumpkin but 5 of those like both, then 2 like only pumpkin. If 8 like apple but 5 of those like both, then only 3 like only apple. So that is 10 students that don't like either.*

Kate made up a Venn Diagram Puzzle. She says there is a way to sort these names. Can you find a way to sort them using the 2-circle Venn Diagrams?

Figure 10.16

Dog   Butterfly   Elephant
Cricket   Rabbit   Beatle
Kangaroo   Tiger   Ant   Ladybug

Explain your thinking.

Students should be able to explain that some are 4 legged animals and some are 6 legged animals. The intersection is all the animals that jump.

The *How Many Animals and Legs?* Problems

These are problems that can be used across the grade levels K–8. There are many different types of these problems with either two or three or sometimes more things to think about (see Figures 10.17 through 10.19). They develop logical thinking and reasoning. They are marvelous problems that can be ramped up as understanding is built. Students should be encouraged to use drawings and tables to show their thinking.

Figure 10.17

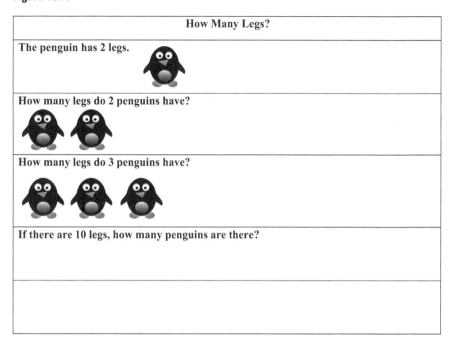

How Many Legs?
The penguin has 2 legs.
How many legs do 2 penguins have?
How many legs do 3 penguins have?
If there are 10 legs, how many penguins are there?

Figure 10.18

Penguins	Legs
1	2
2	4
3	6
?	10
?	?

Figure 10.19

In the zoo yard there are 10 legs. There are penguins and polar bears. How many of each could there be?
In the zoo yard there are 12 legs. There are penguins and polar bears. How many penguins and how many polar bears could there be?
Make up your own penguins and polar bears problem.

Convince Me Problems

Convince me problems are set up so that students can actually prove their thinking in a logical format (see Figure 10.20). These problems require students to use numbers, words and pictures to explain their thinking. They demand that students justify what they know and how they know it. They require students to lay out that justification in an organized manner. Here is an example:

Figure 10.20

Doug said that 5 + 2 is the same as 2 + 5. Convince me that he is correct!

(Convince me with words.)
I know that:

_____

_____

_____

(Convince me with drawings or a diagram.)
I can prove my thinking with a model:

(Convince me with numbers.)
I can verify the answer another way:
Therefore,

Another genre of reasoning problems is where students have to pick which statement is true given a variety of options. This problem really is very centered around comprehension and language (see Figure 10.21).

Figure 10.21

Mike and Mary are having a math discussion. They are talking about which number will make this equation true. Mike says that the answer would be 25. Mary says the answer would be 5.

$15 = ? + 10$

Part A: Who is correct?
Answer: _____

Part B: Explain your thinking with numbers, words and pictures.

Reasoning about Numbers: Greatest Differences or Smallest Sum, etc.

These are problems that are popular abroad in many top performing math countries (see Figures 10.22 and 10.23).

Ted played a game with his friend. In this game they pick cards and then have to make the largest sum. Mary picked 3, 0, 8 and 2. How can she arrange these numbers to get the largest sum?

Figure 10.22
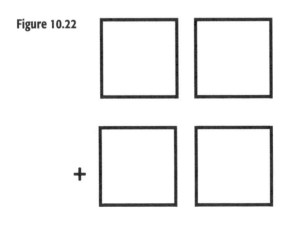

Ricky played a game with his friend. In this game they pick cards and then have to make the largest difference. Miguel picked 5, 8, 7, 1, 0 and 3. How can he arrange these numbers to get the largest difference?

Figure 10.23

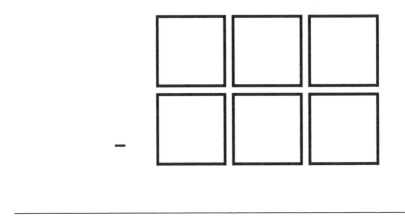

Explain your thinking.

Key Points

- Students should have many opportunities to do pair and group reasoning activities.
- Students should contextualize problems weekly.
- We must focus on set-up and solution equations.
- Graphic organizers help scaffold reasoning.
- Two- or three-bean salad problems help to practice algebraic thinking.
- Coin puzzles help to practice algebraic thinking.
- Concentration matches get students to focus.
- Venn diagrams help students to reason.
- Animal leg problems help students to reason and see patterns.

Summary

We have to teach students to reason. This can be done in really creative, engaging, rigorous ways. Students should be exposed to a variety of activities that scaffold their critical thinking skills. Students should work on matrix problems, Venn diagrams, tables and animal leg problems to improve their reasoning skills. Graphic organizers help to scaffold student thinking through the process. Eventually graphic organizers are faded out and students know how to set up the sketches, tables and diagrams on their own.

Reflection Questions

1. In what ways do you currently do reasoning problems with your students?
2. How often do you ask your students to make up their own word problems? How do you scaffold this so that they are successful?
3. Do you do a variety of types of reasoning problems, including Venn diagrams, table problems, animal leg problems, greatest difference and smallest sum problems?
4. What are 3 big takeaways from this chapter? Where will you start?

References

Kilpatrick, J., Swafford, J. and Findell, B. (Eds.) (2001). *Adding it up: Helping children learn mathematics*. Washington, DC: National Academy Press.

Lawrence Hall of Science. (2007). Three bean salads. Retrieved on December 3, 2016 from http://lawrencehallofscience.org/sites/default/files/247science/mateoc/pdfs/activities_engl/Three_Bean_Salad.pdf.

11

Springboards into Great Word Problem Premises

Math Mentor Texts, Poems, Songs, Shared Experiences and Games

> Word problems don't have to be boring! We must bring the imagination of Disney to the situation at hand. If done right, students can be taught to love word problems like they love good movies.

There are many different ways to get students interested in story problems. Teachers should use math mentor texts, real life stories, poems and shared experiences. All of these types of story starters can be very informative, instructive and engaging. They also serve dual purposes, because you can use them for not only math but also other areas in the curriculum such as science, social studies and even art. There are so many resources available to get you started down this exciting path. In this chapter, I will discuss some of those resources.

Math Mentor Texts

Math mentor texts are picture books that are written with a math premise. There are so many good books out there now, and many of them have been recorded into videos. Use these as springboards into understanding the math through story problems. I have created tables of a few of my favorites (see Figures 11.1 through 11.4). What I truly love about many math mentor texts is now there are tons of math lesson plans that go along with them to help teach the concepts. Furthermore, many have video versions as well. Let's take a look at a few lessons.

Figure 11.1

	Great Math Picture Books		
Math Text	*A Quarter from the Toothfairy* by Caren Holtzman	*My Full Moon Is a Square* by Elinor J. Pinczes	*Actual Size* by Steve Jenkins
Storyline	This is a very funny story about a little boy who gets a quarter from the tooth fairy and goes on a spending spree. But, each time he buys something, he returns it and gets a different combination of a quarter. Well written, humorous and fast-paced.	This story is about a frog who loves to read and the fireflies who love to listen. One night the moon doesn't come out and the fireflies end up saving the day by aligning themselves into square numbers.	This is a magical book that allows different animals to spring out of the pages. It talks about and shows different sizes of animals. Students are mesmerized when they read it.
Online resources	www.k-5mathteachingresources.com/support-files/a-quarter-from-the-tooth-fairy.pdf http://iweb.jackson.k12.ga.us/Exemplars/Math2/pdf/task76.pdf	www.uen.org/Lessonplan/preview.cgi?LPid=18924	www.houghtonmifflinbooks.com/readers_guides/pdfs/JenkinsGuide.pdf
Activities	Have the students find the different ways to make a quarter. http://mathwire.com/literature/toothfairy.pdf	Have the students act out the story by modeling the square numbers with tiles.	Have the students actually measure the animal parts in metric and customary measurements.
Questions to extend the learning:	Coin puzzles: Make 25 cents: Using 3 coins Using 4 coins Using 21 coins	So, if the fireflies came down in a 4 by 4 array, how many fireflies came down? What if it wasn't bright enough and the fireflies had to come down in a 12 by 12 array? Can you model what that would have looked like on the grid paper and solve it?	How many centimeters shorter is the butterfly than the frog? What would a line plot of the length of all these animals look like?

Figure 11.2

Some More Great Math Picture Books by Topic			
Place Value	**Skip Counting**	**Measurement & Data**	**Geometry/Fractions**
Less than Zero by Stuart J. Murphy	*The 512 Ants on Sullivan Street* by Carol Losi	*12 Snails to 1 Lizard* by Susan Hightower	*The Very Greedy Triangle* by Marilyn Burns
Betcha by Stuart J. Murphy	*Two Ways to Count to Ten* by Ruby Dee	*How Many Seeds in a Pumpkin?* by Margaret McNamara	*When a Line Bends* by Rhonda Gowler Greene
A Million Fish...More or Less by Patricia C. McKissack	*How Many Feet in the Bed?* by Deborah Hamm	*Is a Blue Whale the Biggest Thing There Is?* by Robert E. Wells	*Fraction Fun* by David A. Adler
If You Made a Million by David M. Schwartz	*Count on Pablo* by Barbara deRubertis	*Jim and the Beanstalk* by Raymond Briggs	*Gator Pie* by Louisa Matthews
One Is a Snail, Ten Is a Crab by April Sayre	*Double the Ducks* by Stuart Murphy	*The Grouchy Lady Bug* by Eric Carle	*Eating Fractions* by Bruce Mcmillan

Figure 11.3

Math Picture Books About Addition and Subtraction	
Addition	**Subtraction**
Mathterpieces by Greg Tang *Quack and Count* by Keith Baker *12 Ways to Get to 11* by Eve Merriam *Domino Addition* by Lynette Long *Two of Everything* by Lily Toy Hong *Ten Friends* by Bruce Goldston *Each Orange Had 8 Slices: A Counting Book* by Paul Giganti	*How Many Blue Birds Flew Away?* by Donald Crews *Panda Math* by Hua Mei and Mei Sheng *Pete the Cat and His Four Groovy Buttons* by James Dean and Eric Litwin *Five Little Ducks* (song) *Five Little Monkeys* (song) *Ten Sly Piranhas* by William Wise *Construction Countdown* by K.C. Olson

Poems and Songs

There are many different types of songs and poems that teach mathematical concepts. *Songsforteaching.com* has great math songs about a variety of topics. *Canteach.ca* also has some really great poems about money. *Mathstory.com* also has excellent concept poems and songs.

Figure 11.4

Some Great Math Poems and Songs			
Math Text	*One Inch Tall* by Shel Silverstein	*9, Be My Friend* by Carl M. Sherrill	*Numerator Dog* by Mr. R
Storyline	This is a hilarious poem by an all-time great… about being one inch tall.	Great poem about making a 9 into a 10 as a strategy for adding.	This is a very funny poem about a dog that likes to get on top of things.
Online resources	www.marketplace.org/2009/04/27/life/poetry-project/poem-smart-shel-silverstein www.youtube.com/watch?v=y6AITlfWces https://sites.google.com/site/melissacookkindergarten/sample-lesson-plan-page	www.songsforteaching.com/carlsherrill/9bemyfriend.htm	http://mathstory.com/Poems/mydognumerator.aspx#.Vt9aYWQrI6U
Activities	Students can write their own versions of being 1 inch tall and then also extend that conversation to being 1 centimeter tall or 1 decimeter tall.	Have students make a book, using the double 10 frame to illustrate this strategy.	Students then should look at numerators and define and illustrate what they mean.
Questions to extend the learning:	What are 3 things that we can measure in centimeters? What are 3 things that we can measure in inches?	How could we use this strategy with 8 and 7?	Write and illustrate 3 different fractions and explain what the numerators are in these fractions?

Real Life Shared Experiences

Shared experiences are activities that students do to understand and play around with the concepts. For example, every year at one of the schools I worked at in the Bronx, we would have a math Olympics to reinforce measurement concepts. All of the elementary grades participated, and they would get class winners who would then represent them in the finalist competitions. We had wonderful games like, *How far can you blow the cotton ball?* The students had to blow the cotton ball across the table through a straw in 4 puffs. We would then measure how many inches or centimeters they blew their cotton balls. We would have meter jump—which entailed students jumping and then measuring to see who jumped the farthest. It was just a variety of games that were kid-friendly, academically rich and extremely engaging. Since everybody did it, we could then relate to these units of measure and make up problems about them that everyone understood.

The teachers and the students would write word problems about the different events. For example:

1. What is the best unit to measure jumps?
2. If Kelly jumped 10 inches the first jump and 12 inches the next jump, how far did she jump altogether?

Board Game

Students play this board game by reading and solving word problems. (see Figures 11.5 and 11.6). Students pick a card and read it. The answer is on the back. If they get it correct they roll the dice and move that many spaces. If they get the answer wrong, they move 1 space back. Whoever gets to the finish line first wins. For example:

Figure 11.5

Figure 11.6

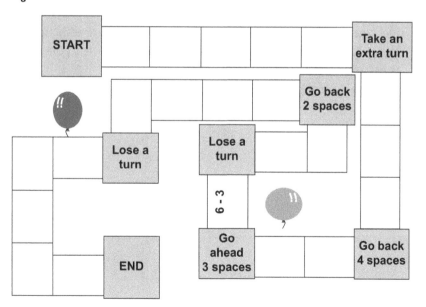

Key Points

- Math mentor texts are great shared experiences.
- Poems and songs can springboard into interesting math topics.
- Shared experiences provide great opportunities to apply the math.
- Games are engaging.

Summary

Getting all students to *love* word problems means that they are working on problems that interest them. Those problems are not necessarily in the textbooks. That is not to say that students shouldn't be able to solve the problems in the textbook. But, they have to learn the math and be able to understand it and be comfortable diving in and pulling it apart in new contexts. So, starting from a place of familiarity boosts engagement and confidence. Confidence with competence makes for success.

Reflection Questions

1. Do you use math mentor texts to enhance and build knowledge around each big idea?
2. Do you use poems and songs to help teach the big ideas?
3. What types of shared experiences do you have with your students that build on their math understandings?
4. What is your biggest takeaway from this chapter?

12

Action Plan

> Problem solving is an integral part of the mathematics learning. In everyday life and in the workplace, being able to solve problems can lead to great advantages (NCTM, 2000).

If you want your students to actually learn how to problem solve, you must have a plan that you implement. That plan consists of several parts, including assessments, a daily routine, guided math lessons, workstations, homework and possibly a schoolwide activity. Below are different templates to help you think about where you are currently and where you want to be (Figures 12.1 through 12.5).

Figure 12.1

Reflection Grid About Problem Solving			
Whole Class Routines	Class Anchor Charts *Good OK Needs Work*	Class Toolkits *Good OK Needs Work*	Problem of the Day *Good OK Needs Work*
Small Group Instruction	Do you have the data to support the work you are doing in small groups? *Good OK Needs Work*	Do you do a variety of activities in your word problem sessions? *Good OK Needs Work*	How do you assess the work you are doing in small groups? What is the immediate feedback that you collect to see if you are accomplishing what you set out to teach and that the students are actually learning what you mean for them to learn? *Good OK Needs Work*
Math Workstations	Individual Work How do you provide for self-assessment? *Good OK Needs Work*	Partner Work How do you scaffold peer editing? *Good OK Needs Work*	Group Work Do your math workstations generally have a variety of activities including word problem sorts, matching/concentration activities, posing and solving problems? *Good OK Needs Work*
Assessment	Do you have individual data on Problem Type Proficiency/levels of students being able to solve the problems? *Good OK Needs Work*	How do you collect ongoing evidence of student achievement throughout the year on problem solving? *Good OK Needs Work*	Are you doing or thinking about doing word problem running records—at least on the students who are exhibiting extreme difficulty? *Good OK Needs Work*
Your own knowledge	CGI Problem Types *Good OK Needs Work*	Various Word Problem Activities *Good OK Needs Work*	Knowledge about getting students to pose/write word problems *Good OK Needs Work*

Figure 12.2

Word Problem Action Planning Mat			
Objectives (List of Objectives)	Tasks (What You Need to Do to Achieve Your Objectives)	Success Criteria (How You Can Identify Your Success)	Time Frame (By When Do You Need to Achieve The Tasks)

Figure 12.3

Goal:			
Strategy:			
What steps must be taken to accomplish this strategy?	What is the timeline?	What resources do you need to do this?	Other notes
1. 2. 3.			

Figure 12.4

Word Problem Solving Action Planning Mat			
Purpose (Mission/Vision)	Current reality/What is the state of the teaching and learning of word problems in your class and school right now?	What are your plans to address these issues?	What do you want to happen? How do you want the reality to be different?
			Where do you want to be in the next year? What does it look like? What does it feel like? How does it sound?

Figure 12.5

Word Problem Checklist

1. Have you assessed the word problem levels of your students so that you can have them working towards proficiency?

2. Do you plan for guided math groups differentiated by the word problem levels that students are working on currently?

3. Are the problems in your word problem workstation leveled?

4. When you introduce a problem do you discuss what type of problem it is?

5. Do you have the students write a set-up equation with the missing part represented with a symbol?

6. Do you rework a problem in different ways throughout the week?

7. Do you encourage the students to explain their work, discussing both their strategies and models?

8. Do you encourage students to always show their work?

FAQs

What should I do to help my kiddos get better at solving word problems?

Solve word problems. Daily, weekly, monthly. I'm serious. There is no magic bullet to teaching students how to solve word problems. It is consistency—which means over time, throughout the year. The emphasis has to be on the practice and process of solving problems rather than on getting the answer. The answer is necessary but not sufficient. We live in a world where students are expected to think about, solve and communicate with each other about different problems.

Is it a daily routine?

It has to be daily. That is a non-negotiable. But daily doesn't mean it takes up the whole day. Don't get sucked into the word problem for the entire math period. Go in, work with it a bit, and come out. Rome wasn't built in a day and neither will problem-solving skills be. But, I promise if you work at it daily, students will learn how to do it well and become very competent and confident problem solvers.

What does the problem-solving workstation look like?

The word problem workstation should have many different activities where students have to think, solve and explain their work. There should be word problems that they have to solve and word problems that they have to write. They should have to check their peers' work. They should play different games where they have to decide what type of word problem it is or what is the most efficient way to answer it. It should have paper and pencil as well as virtual opportunities for students to hone their problem-solving skills.

Do *I* really have to know the problem types?

Yes, Matilda, you do have to know the problem types. You have to know the problem types because you are supposed to be teaching them and if you don't know them then it is going to be a lot harder to teach them. The reason you must learn them is that they actually help you to teach them better and the students to learn them better. It takes the mystery out of problem solving.

We just teach the problems from the book. Do the *kids* really have to know the problem types?

Yes, the students should learn to think about the problems conceptually. The research shows that when students know the problem types they do better because they are focusing and breaking down the problem. They should also be exposed to problems from their everyday lives. They should be writing problems. So workbook problems are just that. They aren't all bad, but they can't carry the whole problem-solving curriculum.

Where do I start?

Start anywhere you feel comfortable. Start small. Start with a whole class daily routine. Start by trying to figure out who knows what in your class. Start by pulling small groups and working with them on the problems they are having trouble with. Yes, do go back and teach one-step problems, if that's what your students need (even if they are in the 5th grade). Hopefully, it'll be quicker and you can get to those multi-step problems with the students understanding what they are doing. Sometimes, we have to slow down to speed up!

How do I monitor progress throughout the year?

Definitely give at least a beginning of the year, middle of the year and end of the year word problem exam. This will at least give you some useful information to navigate your teaching throughout the year.

What about time? There just is not time! How do I do this during *my* math block?

Time is always a question. Cut some ELA time (they usually have double the math block). OK, I digress. You have to make the time to teach problem solving in a planned manner. That means that you must track what you are doing so that you actually get to all the problem types for your grade level during the year. You should make a big problem-solving map/plan for your class, the grade and the school. You have to be very intentional about the homework as well. Always send home some word problems during the week for students to work on. Also, always have a word problem workstation up and running throughout the year.

Reference

National Council of Teachers of Mathematics (NCTM). (2000). *Principles and standards for school mathematics*. Reston, VA: National Council of Teachers of Mathematics.